Samuel Sewall

OF BOSTON

By Ola Elizabeth Winslow:

JOHN BUNYAN

MASTER ROGER WILLIAMS

SAMUEL SEWALL OF BOSTON

Judge Samuel Sewall,
painted by Nathaniel Emmons

Samuel Sewall

OF BOSTON

By Ola Elizabeth Winslow

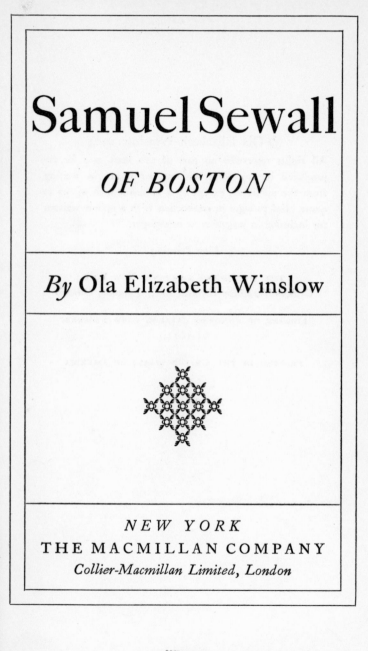

NEW YORK
THE MACMILLAN COMPANY
Collier-Macmillan Limited, London

CONTENTS

PROLOGUE
I

ONE
From These Roots
5

TWO
Orthodox School Days
20

THREE
Harvard College
30

FOUR
New Directions
47

FIVE
Merchant Adventurer
66

v

SIX

'Twas Never So in Boston Before'

79

SEVEN

The English Journey

96

EIGHT

On the Bench in Salem Village

112

NINE

On the Bench in the Superior Court

137

TEN

*Phaenomena Quaedam Apocalyptica
ad Aspectum Novi Orbis Configurata*

152

ELEVEN

The New England Company

157

TWELVE

'The Selling of Joseph'

162

THIRTEEN

Courtships

169

FOURTEEN
Layman of the Old South
182

FIFTEEN
The Diary
193

EPILOGUE
205

NOTES
209

BIBLIOGRAPHICAL NOTE
221

INDEX
225

ILLUSTRATIONS

Judge Samuel Sewall, painted by Nathaniel Emmons

frontispiece

Following page 80:

Boston's First Town-House, burned 1711

The Old Feather Store, Dock Square, Boston

A page from one of Samuel Sewall's Commonplace books

Title page of *Phaenomena quaedam Apocalyptica ad Aspectum Novi Orbis configurata,* 1697

First page of Samuel Sewall's tract, "The Selling of Joseph," 1700

A writ, September 5, 1700, in Judge Sewall's hand

Pages from Samuel Sewall's *Diary*

"Let us serve our Generation according to the Will of God, and afterwards fall asleep."

From SAMUEL SEWALL's Commission with the Boston Train Bands, *May 4, 1691.*

Samuel Sewall
OF BOSTON

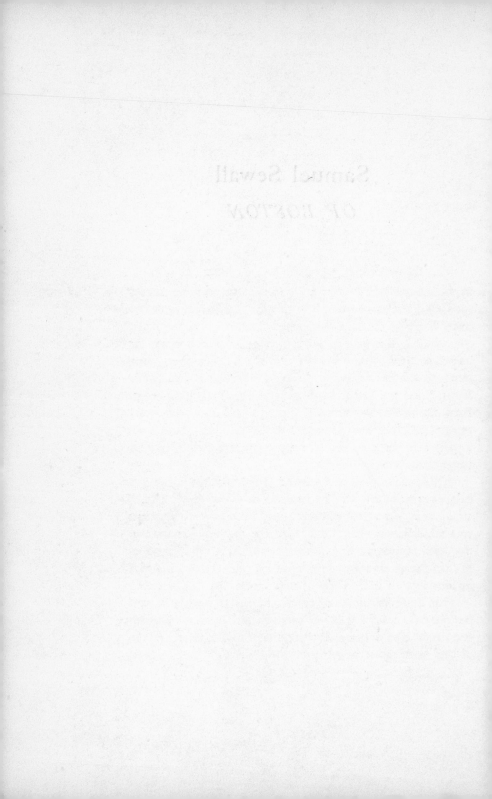

PROLOGUE

IN THE LONG VIEW OF HISTORY, a generation is a brief
span, and yet long enough for its deepest loyalties to become little more than venerated phrases. The dynamic
convictions that impel young men to cross oceans or
march in armies in a year that history remembers, lose
much of their compulsive power as even this same generation becomes adult and new watchwords take over.
Sons honor the traditions of their fathers and pridefully
repeat the familiar phrases, but they find their own
loyalties in the challenge of their own generation. Else
life would never move on.

In successive generations such shifts reshape a nation's
culture and cause life to beat to new rhythms. Much
slips away and is forgotten, and even what remains
wears a different face. One reads the record of change in
the least consequential items of everyday life as well as
in documents of state. Perhaps most clearly one reads it
in the story of individual human lives.

This book attempts to read portions of such a record
for second and third generation New England through
the life of Samuel Sewall of Boston. His share in the life
of his own generation was long enough and varied

enough to represent many different interests and attitudes. He was magistrate, churchman, judge, merchant,
had his hand in the affairs of the college, of the military,
and in various other aspects of New England life. Extant records show some impact of his thought and action
in them all. He was consulted, listened to, and though
often opposed, was seldom ignored. Because he was not
an original thinker, his thought was more representative
than if it had taken paths yet undiscovered and as yet
untrodden by the many. Characteristically, it lay along
the main highways of thought in his time, reflecting its
inner urges more completely than he might have cared
to think, for in his own eyes he was carrying the banners
of "our Fathers before us."

For later generations his story is an open book. Record
of his outer life is generously preserved in official files of
town, of court, of church, college, and in registers of
ships, cargoes, sailings, merchant enterprises by land
and sea. Better still, his springs of action are revealed in
his day to day diary, intended for no eyes but his own.
His secret hopes and ambitions, his confessions, waver-
ings, superstitions, prayers and beliefs; all are there,
and to a wealth unmatched in the life record of almost
any other man of his time in New England.

His American life began almost precisely with the
second generation. In midsummer 1661, when as a boy
just turned nine he was "carried out in arms" from the
Prudent Mary in Boston Harbor, the Massachusetts
Bay Colony, where he would spend nearly sixty-nine
more years, was thirty-one years old, a generation of
time. Only a few of the first generation were still living.
John Winthrop, leader of the first migration, had been
asleep in what is now King's Chapel churchyard for
twelve years. Most of his companion passengers in his
flagship, the *Arbella*, were gone also. Of the three other

men who had stood with him under the great tree by the waterside to "take the covenant" which had created the First Church of Boston, only John Wilson was left. He had six more years in which to fight the countercurrents already at work in his congregation, of which the majority were now New England born. John Cotton, who had bidden the vanguard of the 1630 migration farewell and godspeed on the other side and had rejoined them later in the New England Boston, had been silent for nearly a decade. Harvard College was now twenty-five years old. In the words of the little booklet *New England's First Fruits*, published in the seventh year after its founding, the time when "our present ministers shall lie in the Dust" had almost turned fact. Their lives were fast becoming a memory. It was a new day.

Samuel Sewall's generation would also be pioneers, but it would be pioneering with a difference. First generation leaders had felt themselves called to act in a vast cosmic drama. The work they had undertaken, as John Winthrop had told them in his *Arbella* sermon, was more God's design than their own. To their younger successors this unexampled privilege had become a sermon admonishment, grown paler with many repetitions. The bitter uncertainties of the 1620's and 1630's would not be repeated. New England would not only survive; she was beginning to prosper. To pledge one's self to maintain what an earlier generation has established asks a different degree of surrender, a different intensity of dedication, and a far different courage. There is only one first time. The 1630 days were now a page in history. Samuel Sewall would belong to a generation that had not lived them. As a nine-year-old boy he came into a ready-made world. Men he did not know had made it. His generation would shape what they found for a future day they too would never know.

From These Roots

MEMORIES of a nine-year-old are likely to be scant and perhaps inconsequential, especially when summoned nearly a lifetime later. Samuel Sewall's memory of the day he left his English birthplace and early boyhood home in Hampshire for the New World was somewhat buttressed by the fact that this day had also been an historic day for England. "I remember being at Bishop Stoke and Badesly [he wrote] April 23, 1661. the day of the Coronation of K. Charles 2ᵈ." "The Thunder and Lightening of it" had marked the day in his boy memory, as also for Samuel Pepys, Richard Baxter and others who were not boys barely past their ninth birthdays. As mature men they had been concerned lest this fearsome storm be an ill omen.

The boy Samuel remembered also that after the thunder and lightning he had gone with his mother, his two brothers, two sisters, and also John Nash and Mary Hobs, his mother's servants, to Winchester, home of her close relatives, to "be in a readiness for the Pool Waggons" carrying their possessions. Of the family farewells there, he recalled only the tears of "my very worthy and pious Uncle Mr. Stephen Dummer," and boylike, "the

Raisins and Almonds" bestowed by Captain Dummer
of Swathling. Thereafter mother, children and servants
had gone to Pumpyard, London, to wait for "the going
of the Ship," the *Prudent Mary*, which lay at Graves-
End. This land journey from Bishop Stoke, Sewall's
birthplace, to London was about eighty miles in a south-
westerly direction toward Southampton.

He recalled nothing of the land journey or of the
embarking, only that at Dover sheep were taken on
board, a last remembered event before the long eight-
week voyage, with "nothing to see but Water and the
Sky." His memory preserved only the fear that "I
should never get to Shoar again." Logic helped out,
however, even at a bare nine years, and he reasoned that
Captain Woodgreen and the Mariners "would not have
ventured themselves if they had not hopes of getting
to Land again." After eight weeks hopes were fulfilled,
land came in sight, and he reported being "overjoyed."
The guns at Castle Island fired in salute, the ship's gun
replied, and on Lord's Day, the boat being grounded,
he was "carried out in arms."

A new home awaited him. "My Father hastened to
Boston and carried his Family to Newbury by Water in
Mr. Lewis," he wrote. The last sentence of his remembered voyage to the New World reads, "Mr. Ordway
carried me ashore in his Canoe." At Newbury, July 6,
1661, it was still a day of small things.

Had he searched his memory still more sharply, as he
wrote this account in his sixty-eighth year, he might
have recalled other details in the long anticipation of
this journey. His father, Henry Sewall, Jr. had been
absent from home for nearly two years, making preparations in Newbury for permanent settlement there, and
while his mother awaited the summons to rejoin him she

had busied herself with the manifold preparations such a move required. There were five young children: Hannah, the eldest, aged twelve, Samuel next at nine, John not yet seven, Stephen not yet four, and Jane, born since her father's departure in 1659.

America had been in the family thought much longer than Henry Sewall's 1659 journey. He had first come as a boy of twenty, when his father, also Henry Sewall by name, "out of dislike to the English Hierarchy" had sent his only son to New England with "net Cattel and Provisions sutable for a new Plantation." [1] During the twenty-seven years since then, Henry Sewall, Jr. had divided his life almost equally between Old England and New.

For his son Samuel's story, it is important to remember that the original impulse back of this family migration had been economic, not religious, and this in spite of the fact that it had belonged to the years when escape from Laudian strictures was a determining motive in early Massachusetts settlement. Henry Sewall, Sr. was a wealthy landholder in the Coventry region of Warwickshire. He was of Saxon heritage. Apparently shrewd in business, he was looking toward New England for financial advantage, not for freedom from ritualistic worship. His action was not hasty, nor was it his alone. Shortly after the sailing of the Winthrop fleet in 1630, he had joined with Sir Richard Saltonstall, Richard and Stephen Dummer of Hampshire, and several wealthy men of Wiltshire, in the forming of a company for the raising and exportation of cattle, sheep and horses in the New World. The site chosen was the fertile pasture land along the Quascacunquen River, and the time, shortly after the sailing of the *Mary and John*, which had brought the nucleus of the Newbury settlement

under the leadership of Thomas Parker and James
Noyes, ministers.

At this early date Henry Sewall, Sr. had not yet made
his own decision to emigrate, as his associate Richard
Dummer had done two years earlier, and as he himself
would do later. Instead, he had charged his twenty-year-
old son with responsibility for his share in the cattle-
raising project. It was a stern assignment for so young
a man, the son of a wealthy father, and with probably
his short lifetime of protection behind him from every
form of such hardship as New England would offer.
The previous conditions of young Henry's life are not
known, or even his residence, but it is likely to have
been in the Coventry region, which had been the Sewall
seat during the two generations preceding Henry Sewall,
Sr. There were many Sewalls in this neighborhood, their
names spelled also Seawall, Sewell, Shewall, Shewel
and Shewell. The choice of cattle raising as Henry
Sewall's New World project would suggest some acquaintance with animal husbandry or farming, but no
such evidence is on the record. We know only that in the
fall of 1634 Henry Sewall, Jr. set sail in the *Elizabeth
and Dorcas*, bringing English servants, neat cattle,
equipment and provisions suitable for a new plantation.
The voyage must have been a grim experience, as thirty
of the passengers died of a tropical fever and were buried
at sea. One of them, Edward Bosworth, being "ready
to dye, ask'd to be carried upon the Deck, that he might
see Canaan. When he had seen the Land, he resigned
his Soul, and dyed: was carried ashoar and buried in
Boston." [2] Not a scene to forget, even in one's own release from the long voyage, and with the earth beneath
his feet once more. In family tradition, reported by
Samuel Sewall, John Cotton invited Henry Sewall to

settle in Boston, where presently the pulpit might once
more have claimed him, but "in regard of his Cattel, he
chose to go to Newbury." The phrasing catches the eye,
for in Samuel Sewall's story there is something of a
parallel. In regard to cattle of a different sort, he too
in his twenties turned from the pulpit to a secular life.

According to a phrase on his tombstone, Henry Sewall
"winter'd in Ipswich" (then called Agawam), and when
spring broke, "helped begin" the plantation at Newbury, first called Quascacunquen for the river on whose
banks the earliest settlement was established. The
Parker and Noyes company, which landed in the fall of
1634 and picked the site for the town, had also wintered
in Ipswich. Tradition brought them also in the early
spring of 1635, by water, through Plum Island Sound
and up the Great River, now Parker River, to the site
they had chosen on the northern bank. In town records
this part of the town is spoken of as the Lower Green,
later as Old Town Green. The first houses and the
meetinghouse were built at this point. A winding foot-
path and horseback trail through the woods already con-
nected Ipswich with Newbury.

On May 6, 1635, a General Court action named
Quascacunquen as a plantation, giving the court power
to see that the "said plantation shall receive a sufficient
company to make a competent towne." This result was
soon assured, as new settlers came on every ship, 1635
being a peak year for immigration. At the same court "it
was ordered that Mr. [Richard] Dummer and Mr.
Bartholomew shall set out a convenient quantity of land
within the bounds of Newberry, for the keeping of the
sheep and cattle that came over in the Dutch shipps this
yeare, and to belong to the owners of said cattle." [3]
Henry Sewall, Jr. was one of these owners. On the allot-

ment of land as ordered he was granted five hundred acres, John Clark four hundred, Richard Dummer three hundred and John Spencer a mill-lot of fifty acres. These allotments were proportionate to the amount each adventurer had put into the common stock, the rate being two hundred acres for every £50, £50 for every person he had transported, and £50 for himself. At this same session Richard Dummer and John Spencer were given "liberty to build a mill and weire at the falls of Newberry." Previously Richard Dummer had built a mill at Roxbury, where he first "sat down" in 1633.

The cattle-raising enterprise did not long survive as a group project, for in November, 1635, because of the negligence of Thomas Colman, brought over by the investors for the "keeping of certain horses, bulls, and sheep in a general stock for the space of three years," [4] the gentlemen concerned were directed to "divide the oats and hay provided for said cattell among themselves, and soe every one take care of their own during the winter." Thereafter each man was his own keeper. As statute required, the owners lived in Newbury within one-half mile of the meetinghouse.

Loss of the town records before 1637 leaves many blanks in the story of the first three years. It was a story written afresh by each new settlement, of land cleared, houses built, crops planted, town and church organized, the story of alternate hope and discouragement, gain and loss, resourcefulness sometimes too severely tested, of triumph and failure, and always somewhere the story of tragedy. Henry Sewall's share in these earliest Newbury experiences went unrecorded, except for additional grants of land to him as the cattle raising prospered, his name in the list of those made freemen, once of his walking to Cambridge on the hotly contested election day in 1637 to cast his vote for John Winthrop instead of Sir Harry Vane, and of his own repeated service as deputy to the General Court. The only item against him on the books is a twelve penny fine for absence from town meeting on one occasion. Other than for these bare items, we know him as a son and father in his own son's record only, and this too scant of detail to permit a full scale portrait.

After what looks like a successful beginning, with permanent residence assured, and twelve years of pioneering behind him, Henry Sewall, upon his marriage to Jane Dummer, daughter of his associate Stephen Dummer, returned in 1646 to England with his nineteen-year-old bride and her parents, Stephen and Alice Dummer. In family tradition, reported by Samuel Sewall,[5] the reason for this change was the unwillingness of the elder Dummers to spend another winter in New England, "the Climat being not agreeable," and either through her own desire, or that of her parents for her, Jane decided to go with them. Warrant for their departure is easy enough to find, in addition to the winter rigors. The mid-forties were times of low spirits for New Englanders. Immigration had all but ceased because of English hopes born of Civil War victories, and many Massachusetts settlers were returning to the Mother Country. Prices for cattle had fallen from twenty-five pounds to five or six. There was no money, corn being the usual medium of exchange. June, 1646, had brought "innumerable armies of caterpillars" ruinous to the crops until, in answer to prayer [so we read], "God took them away." For all of these reasons, or possibly for none of them, Stephen and Alice Dummer left Newbury permanently. Richard Dummer went later, but returned to New England before his death.

That this return to England meant a difficult new start for thirty-two-year-old Henry Sewall, would seem to be clear from the record of his various changes of residence during the next thirteen years. He and his bride lived briefly first at Warwick, at Tunworth, where Hannah, their first child, was born, in Bishop Stoke, former seat of the Dummers, and after 1653 in North Baddesley, where Henry Sewall served as minister. Of this seemingly strange shift to the pulpit, nothing survives but the fact. No record of University training to the end of ministry has come to light, but as this was the period of Cromwellian relaxation in strict clerical training, a candidacy at North Baddesley may have been acceptable without it. Also during the residences at Warwick, Tunworth or Bishop Stoke, he may have been pursuing studies toward a preaching career.

In New England, Henry Sewall had been a church member, presumably a man of religious faith, but nothing in his son's later references to him suggests the man of books or of pastoral concern. What we know of him after this ministerial period would indicate that preaching was a fortuitous choice rather than one shaped by natural leaning or professional training. Our knowledge stops with the fact. It was a chapter of brief duration, as also in his son's life. For both men the secular triumphed over the churchly, but in both lives the pulpit is at least on the record.

During the North Baddesley residence, Henry Sewall made two trips back to Newbury, one in 1650 to visit his father, Henry Sewall, Sr. and another in 1659; the occasion for the second trip being his father's death and the responsibility for settling his considerable estate. On this second trip he brought with him a letter from Richard Cromwell, Protector, dated from Whitehall, March 23,

1658/59, naming Henry Sewall as a man "laborious
and industrious in the work of the ministry, and very
exemplary for his holy life," and asking that he might
have "speedy justice done him concerning the said estate,
that he may return the sooner to his ministerial charge
in North Baddesley." [6] Whether Henry Sewall's decision not to return was already made before this neces-
sary journey, is not indicated, but so it came about. He
remained in Newbury for the forty-one years he had
still to live.

His decision is understandable. His father's large
holdings in land and cattle were now his own. They
demanded attention. His own rents when remitted to
him during his absence had come to very little. By continuing the absence he might lose all. He had spent
twelve of his younger years in Newbury and this 1659
trip was in a sense a return home. His wife Jane had
also lived here from her thirteenth to her nineteenth
year, so that she, like her husband, had roots in New
England. At this date she was thirty-four and her husband was forty-six. Three more children would be born
to them in Newbury: Anne, Mehitable and Dorothy.
The five English-born ones, Hannah, Samuel, John,
Stephen and Jane, were still too young for their English
heritage to be other than a dim memory. New England
would soon claim them all for her own.

Samuel Sewall had never seen his grandfather Henry
Sewall, Sr. who had lived only five years after this first
grandson was born, and whatever he had been told about
him, wealth would probably have been part of the story.
Moreover, the evidence was visible to the eye in the
considerable pasture lands that spread out from the
Newbury settlement. His home stood on the Lower
Green. Extant Newbury records tell little of him except

that on several occasions his irascible temper brought him unfortunate notice. Once it was sharp words with John Winthrop, Jr. over certain land limits; once "contemptuous speeche and carriage to Mr. Saltonstall" which put him under bond for good behavior in £66 13s 4d. At another time he disturbed the congregation on Sabbath, and on still another drew blood in an Ipswich town meeting, an offence for which he made public confession.[7] In the will of his mother Margaret (Grazenbrook) Sewall there is a passage suggesting that such behaviors had a long history. She wrote,

"And I doe forgive unto Henry Sewall, my eldest son, his offences wherein and whereby he hath sundry times offended me, beseeching Almighty God to give him a heart to deal conscionably with his brother and his sisters, as he would be done to, unto whom I give, I mean to my said son, twelve pence in money."[8]

His father's will also contains a proviso "in trust and confidence that he doe with all humilite acknowledg his former offences against his mother, before my overseers, to her content, and afterwards to continue obedient." From what details are known, he failed to do so, contested his mother's will through long litigation, but in the end did not succeed in breaking it.

During the long Newbury dispute over whether to move the meetinghouse from the Lower Green, Grandfather Henry was one of the stoutest opposers; and when his side finally lost, he gave his property to his son, and moved across the river to Rowley, where he lived until his death. He is buried there. Only in the fact of his thirteen years' residence and his original investments in cattle and provisions is he a New Englander. Samuel Sewall, his grandson, was more a second generation immigrant than a third, in terms of his family's constructive share during Newbury's pioneering years.

Whatever survived concerning the still earlier Sewalls, as the young Samuel heard it, would probably have echoed the story of wealth and prosperity. Before grandfather Henry Sewall there had been great-grandfather Henry Sewall, a linen-draper of Coventry. "He acquired a great Estate, and was more than once chosen Mayor of the City," family tradition reported. He was buried in the Draper's Chapel of St. Michael's Church in Coventry. His brother William Sewall had also been mayor, a detail of prominence which Samuel Sewall repeated pridefully in the family record he prepared for his son. The fact that in this record he made no mention of the family crest described by Thomas Fuller as being borne by John Sewall of Essex and Herts in 1387 probably means that it did not belong to the Sewalls of Coventry. Three centuries later it was assigned to the Sewalls of Northampton and Sewall of the Isle of Wight. Samuel Sewall of Boston made no use of it, as his dignity as Chief Justice would have permitted, had a family claim to it existed. It shows three gadbees, divided by a chevron, with another bee above. The coat of arms borne by John de Savelle, who accompanied Richard the Black Prince into Aquitaine, shows butterflies instead of gadbees, a change which might be interpreted as evidence that the Sewalls of New England did not belong to the heraldic family. *The Visitation of Warwickshire, 1619*, identified Grandfather Sewall only as Henry Sewall of Coventry.[9]

On the maternal side the heritage can be traced somewhat further back and is a shade more illustrious. From early in the twelfth century there was great wealth, an occasional title, and rather frequent public office for the

Dummers. The English ancestry can be traced un-
brokenly to Henry de Domera, living in 1107–1128.
The branch of the Dummer family that united with the
Sewalls was descended from John Dommer of Overton,
Hants, whose daughter Matilda, great-grandmother of
Richard and Stephen Dummer, had married Richard
Pyldrym of Owlesbury and Overton, Hants. Thomas
Pyldrym Dummer of Bishop Stoke, their grandson, was
the ancestor of whom Samuel Sewall wrote,

"Of my Parents Eight Children, it fell to my share only to
be born in the parish where my Great Grandfather liv'd
and to be baptised in the Church where he lies interd." [10]

In the generation of Richard and Stephen Dummer, the
name Pyldrym was dropped and the name Dummer
resumed.

Material prosperity continued for both Richard and
Stephen in New England. Richard Dummer was the
wealthiest man in Newbury during his residence there
and perhaps in the whole colony. His allotment of 1,080
acres of Newbury land and the pasturage of sixty cows
in the common pasture was matched by his continued
generosity, extended not to Newbury neighbors alone.
Once it went "in a private way" to John Winthrop at the
time of the loss of his estate, once to the town of Boston
in a time of need.

During the Anne Hutchinson crisis in 1637 Richard
Dummer sympathized with the Hutchinson faction, was
condemned by the court, turned out of his post as deputy
to the General Court, and disarmed for his "erroneous
opinions." He went back to England for a time, but returned to America in the following year and henceforth
kept his opinions to himself. After his return he served
again as Representative in 1640, 1645, and 1647. There

was a ministerial chapter in the Dummer family story also, but it came in later generations. Richard Dummer's son Jeremiah was one of the notable clergymen of his time. It was the wealth of his son William, Lieut. Governor of Massachusetts, which endowed Dummer Academy.

Not a highly distinguished ancestry, so far as it is known, but on both the Sewall and the Dummer sides it shows men and women of character as well as substance. The three-known Henry Sewalls were all men of wealth, education, breeding, and civic mindedness. Like the Dummers, they belonged to the solid gentry, middle-class men of the "country party" group that produced Cromwell, Hampden, and many other mid-century English leaders in church and state. In the flux of English society during this period it was the middle-class group that was pushing upward most successfully and creating a new aristocracy of wealth and political power. The later generations were of non-conforming sympathies but without extravagance of zeal. Religion for the earlier Sewalls and Dummers alike was a minor strain, less dominant than the economic, but sufficient to balance a heritage in which this earthly world was abundantly important.

Recognizing that a man's life begins long before his birth; in fact, as far back as his progenitors can be summoned, one may see in this incomplete Sewall and Dummer ancestral record various items that seem significant for the Boston Samuel Sewall. Back of him on both sides was the confidence born of economic security and the social standing that security carries with it. He could take these assurances for granted. There was also the dignity belonging to civil office and the sense of obligation such office imposed. These were qualities he possessed and used significantly throughout his life.

His earliest memories belonged to the ministerial years of his father in the North Baddesley household, where certain patterns of behavior would have been established beyond easy abandonment. Prayer and Bible reading would have been as certain a part of the day's program as the morning milk and porridge, and he would hardly have known that all men did not pray and go to service. The authority of the Ten Commandments would have been unquestioned and the Old Testament patriarchs would have been as real as the English kings. Sunday would have been a day like no other of the seven, with sermons and psalm-singing a part of the difference. Aged nine, when he arrived in Newbury, he would already have a foundation and a scaffolding on which the more rigorous New England emphasis on religion could build. Looking back on his own history from his churchgoing maturity, it pleased him to know that

"The light of the Lord's Day was the first light that my Eyes saw, being born a little before day-break."

The date was March 28, 1652.

"I was baptised by Mr. Rashly [he added] in Stoke Church, May 4, 1652. Mr. Rashly first preached a Sermon, and then baptised me. After which an entertainment was made for him and many more." [11]

The treasured fact of birth on the Sabbath naturally enough bore the New England stamp, but North Baddesley had provided hospitable soil for its roots.

As a nine-year-old immigrant, he would not long remember much of his native Hampshire, a countryside of quiet beauty, undramatic of nature's gift, but a rich center of English history: Roman roads, walls, strange earthworks, suggestive of far antiquity. The green mounds of Basingstoke had probably been thrown up by the Celts centuries before his birth. Cromwell's Ironsides had marched and galloped down the High Road, where now the tracks of the Southeastern Railroad run. The Great Chalk Pit, still known as Oliver's Delve, had been occupied by Southampton troopers during the siege that reduced Basing House, "Loyalty House" of the Cavaliers, to ruin. The present west window of Winchester cathedral had not yet been made of fragments of glass swept up after Cromwell's destruction of the earlier window. The church of North Baddesley, where his father preached, stood according to tradition, on the site of a heathen temple. Knights Hospitalers had kept a preceptory there after the twelfth century. Perhaps they had planted the ancient fig trees surrounding the church. Romsey, where he went to school, had grown into a town from the one-time abbey of Benedictine nuns in the fair valley of the River Test.[12] As a nine-year-old boy he would have heard stories of these long ago associations many times, but all such tales would soon lie vague and deep in his memory. Adventures of his earliest days in Newbury, tales of Indians and wolves took over to be his day by day romance. He was young enough to grow up almost a complete New Englander, with only seeming half-true reminders of his English beginnings.

Orthodox School Days

H IS ENGLISH educational foundations were perhaps his most lasting debt to the motherland. On the anniversary of his landing date in Newbury years later he wrote,

"This day it is Fifty four years Since I first was brought ashoar to Boston near where Scarlet's wharf now is, July, 6, 1661, Lord's Day. . . . The Lord help me to Redeem the Time which passes so swiftly. I was then a poor little School-boy of Nine years and ¼ old." [1]

Right: as the son of only a short-term minister, he had been "born to be educated," and the process began early. The beginnings were in North Baddesley, where "by the merciful goodness of God" he was taught to read. This was probably training in a dame school, which by the time he was seven would have made him eligible for the Grammar School at Romsey, where he reported being taught by "Mr. Figes." Romsey was only three and one-half miles from North Baddesley, but with transportation probably by horseback, far enough to have made him a boarding pupil.

Nothing is known about "Mr. Figes" except his name, but if his training were standard, Latin would have received first emphasis. English Grammar School masters found it "extreme vexation" to be "toiled amongst such little Petties" as had not yet put their "Abcie and Primer" far enough behind them to be able to read *Matthew, Mark, Luke,* and *John* without stumbling. Thus grounded, they were counted ready to begin Latin not only on the printed page, but for instruction from the master's desk and for conversation during school hours. The school day was long, the discipline insistent, with penalties at every false step, so that after two years with Mr. Figes, eleven-year-old Samuel should have been already an initiate in Latin, the first of the "Tongues" to be attacked in the long path ahead.

Arrived in Newbury, he was immediately put under the tutelage of the "Reverend and excellent Mr. Thomas Parker," pastor of the church, who would prepare him for Harvard College. Another teacher from nine to fifteen might have shaped his potentialities to other ends or at least shaped them differently, but after six years in the schoolroom of the Parker–Noyes house just across the lane from the first Sewall residence, the Parker standard and direction were ineradicable. In many ways, fortunately so. At this date there was no town Grammar School in Newbury, still a small settlement of less than the fifty householders needful to make a public Grammar School a legal requirement. A vote to establish one had been on the town book since 1647/ 48, but it did not become fact until 1675. Meanwhile Thomas Parker's school kept the English ideal of education before every parent and freeman, even those whose sons would not have been able to qualify for college entrance. In this school there would be no break in Samuel Sewall's training according to standards of preparation for Harvard.

There were only twelve or fourteen boys in the school, chosen from those designed for the ministry by their parents. Thomas Parker took no pay for teaching them, regarding his schoolroom labors as part of his service to the church for which he lived. His particular genius as a teacher would seem to have been his success in encouraging boys at this early age to go beyond the lessons of the day. He was particularly concerned also (this a personal quirk) that they make verses, in Latin and English, as some of them continued to do throughout life, Samuel Sewall among them. Thomas Parker's discipline was gentle as to "school-faults." There was little correction and little punishment, except for *lying* and *fighting* — "Crimes" he would not endure.

In any time or place Thomas Parker would have been one man among many; and in frontier Newbury, to which he and James Noyes, his cousin, had led the first settlers in 1634, and ministered to them twice a week through twenty-seven years, he was, in 1661 almost a patriarch. He was also beginning, in sequel to his long leadership, to demand rather too insistently what he considered the prerogatives of his station, and losing both peace of mind and affection thereby. His long controversy with the covenated membership over their share in the management of church affairs (which in his view was no share at all) was already under way. This "trouble" would agitate the whole community until his death, split the church and town into factions, call church councils, invite legal action, but never really be settled at all. Strong preacher that he was, in the administration of a church community he was short-sighted almost to blindness. He shared the current skepticism of many leaders, churchly and civil, as to the democratic process, and the battle would be long.

Outside of Newbury, he was known chiefly for his learning, and no doubt had sometimes heard himself called the most learned man in New England. It was of course learning within the limits of theology, ancient times and tongues. His own education had been varied to a degree beyond that of most of his ministerial colleagues in New England, had given him a wider range of acquaintance and, one might think, also of experience. It had taken him to Magdalen College (Oxford), to Trinity College (Dublin), to Leyden, where he had studied with William Ames, thence to Franeker University in the Netherlands, where he had taken the degree of Doctor of Philosophy in 1617. Ironically enough for one who became so thoroughly orthodox, his 70 *Theses*, published when he was twenty-two years old, had put him under strong suspicion of heresy, but he was finally cleared at the Council of Dort through the able defence of William Ames.[2]

Prior to his migration to New England, he had kept a school in his native Wilts, and upon coming to Newbury in 1634, had transferred the English model entire to the new settlement. James Noyes, who had been a co-teacher in Wilts, had become teacher in the Newbury meetinghouse. He had died in 1656, but his family still occupied the house in which the school was kept. Long before Samuel Sewall became a pupil in it, Thomas Parker had made a name for himself in Harvard circles for the thoroughness of his training, and the success of his boys in the Yard. Six years hence, Samuel Sewall, aged fifteen, would have his chance to continue this distinction.

By being enrolled at the age of nine, he was already "elected" thus early to scholarship of the erudite English pattern, chiefly in the Tongues. Also, Thomas

Parker would kindle in him a lifelong interest in biblical prophecy by strictly literal interpretation, encourage the habit of using a sharp-edged line-and-rule measurement for conduct, and by his own example foster also a stern conservatism. This venerable teacher, before whom the young boy sat for six formative years, communicated not only something of Thomas Parker himself, but also much of the first generation concept of the God of the Hebrews and the symmetry of the world He had created; not religion as an unfolding experience in each individual life, but the biblical word unchanged by a syllable as a mandate for living. By the conditions of his admission, Samuel Sewall was also committed, at least by acknowledged parental hope, to the ministry as his lifetime work, and one may be sure he was not allowed to forget it in the classroom. Small wonder then that to turn to secular employment later, either through his own desire or through counsel that he trusted, sent him into the confusion and distress of his early twenties.

Schooldays over for the week, on Sundays he sat with the other village boys in the pew designed for them and under the watching eye of Giles Cromwell (or his equivalent), who by town vote "was to keep the boys in order in the meetinghouse, and to give notice to selectmen of such as are out of order, and to have six shillings for his paynes." [3] Those of the boys who were in the Parker school must take sermon notes for the report expected of them as they stood before the master on Monday morning — text, doctrine, and its development point by point to the end.

Apart from the schoolroom on weekdays and the meetinghouse pew on Sunday, life in Newbury during the 1660's would have been life in a strange world to a boy with Latin in his head. But not for long. The wide spaces stretching in all directions would soon replace the chalk downs and gentle slopes of Hampshire, which was also a land spare of human habitation. The town of Newbury embraced a five-mile area, but at this date, for safety, each house stood on its four-acre town plot. Henry Sewall's land bordered on the main street, but his house stood at the far corner of his land apart from the meetinghouse. Years later he built a larger house not far from this first site.

Out of anyone's windows the town pasture, the ox and calf common, the sheep range were visible. There were more cattle and sheep than men, women, and children. To see the herdsmen pen the sheep and cattle for the night was an event to boy eyes, always the same, always different, and always coming to the expected end. What lay beyond these fields, this village? Not a stretch of Roman road, ancient churches, castles, perhaps a cathedral. Instead the endless sea, the woods, also seemingly endless, and filled with unknown dangers of which every child was warned and then warned again for the thousandth time. Of the natural beauty of this yet unspoiled land, hardly a word in print during these years of autumn glory in these woods and swamps, not even for eyes that had never before looked on New England maples. Maybe there were words spoken when October spread the glory before them. But these wide spaces, this landscape as nature offered it, would be the most cherished landscape of Samuel Sewall's life. He would possess these grazing fields and these empty miles as he would possess no other of the hundreds of acres he would presently own by legal deed.

The meetinghouse, which except for the Noyes homestead was the nearest building to the Sewall home, would be during his boyhood the center of village life, as in any town of these early generations. In 1661, when he came, the second building was being built, close to the smaller first structure, in which Sunday worship was still being held. In the preceding January, Henry Jaques had been chosen by the selectmen to build a gallery at both ends and along the west side. He was to fell the timber, provide all the "stuffe," and to make "three payre of stairs," his pay to be "thirty pounds in good current pay or provisions," together with all the "old stuffe of the old gallery in the old meetinghouse." [4] Presumably this construction was almost completed by midsummer. Seats had been assigned in June, and there was the usual muttered displeasure in some quarters about the places designated. Later, when the building was in use, there would be occasional usurpation on Sunday morning of a more desirable seat, with consequent confusion if not loud voices and blows. It was always so. The wolfheads on the door were bringing forty shillings for the killers in 1661, and also providing more eloquent warning by their large numbers than the thousandth counsel to the children to stay away even from the edges of the dark woods.

Even Sundays were not all sermon admonition to piety, psalm-singing, prayer while the congregation stood for perhaps an hour or longer, noon interval and back to another sermon. Sometimes Sunday, in addition, provided drama. On one occasion in 1663, when Samuel Sewall was eleven years old, Lydia Wardwell not only disrupted the Sunday preaching, but made front-page conversation for days afterward. She had come unclothed into the meetinghouse, to answer by this exhibition those who had accused her of teaching false doctrine. Described as a "young and tender chaste woman," she had withdrawn from Newbury church and though often sent for to give her reasons for separating, she had refused to do so. Her unseemly arrival on Sunday morning had been a *sign* of her non-compliance. In punishment, by order of the Court, she had been tied to the fencepost of Steven Swett's tavern and sorely lashed with "a certain twenty or thirty cruel stripes" while her judges looked on from the tavern.[5]

On another Sunday in his young manhood, Samuel Sewall recorded a similar exhibition in his diary, as "the Greatest and most amazing Uproar that I ever saw." This had been in the Old South Church of Boston. Margaret Brewster, a Quaker, had come into service "in a Canvas Frock, her hair disshevelled and loose like a Periwigg, her face as black as ink, led by two other Quakers, and two followed behind." She had left her precious shoes and stockings in the church porch in care of John Easton.[6]

On another boyhood day in Newbury, the eleven-year-old who would one day be Chief Justice of Massachusetts Province might have been present when Elizabeth Webster stood at the meetinghouse door "from the ringing of the first bell until the minister be ready to begin prayer, with a paper on her head written in capital letters FOR TAKING A FALSE OATH IN COURT." She had been given the choice of so doing or of paying the accustomed fine of fifteen pounds and being henceforth disabled from taking an oath. The humiliation of standing thus placarded and gazed upon by her neighbors had seemed to her the lesser penalty.[7]

As always in such items, town books find little occasion to record harmonious living, but enter the misdemeanors, which may quite belie the spirit of life as it was lived, much as they illuminate the picture. The recorded cases against law and order in Newbury open

wide vistas for these early years. In 1662 the first jail
break "of its kind committed in the whole country" may
be one of these. A prisoner securely fastened inside, the
door locked, the "hasp put on to the staple on the
outsyde of the dore, which none within can unhasp,
did that night break prison." His neighbor, as was presently discovered, had "un-hasped the dore on the outside," and let him out. Constables, as well as other
prisoners, learned by this much talked of offence.[8]

In the year 1661 on the pages of a neighboring town
book one reads,

"It is ordered yt if any person shall discharge a gunn in the
meetinghouse, or any other house without leave of the
owner or house holder, hee or they shall forfeit five shillings for every such offence nor shall any person ride or
lead a horse into the meetinghouse under a like penalty." [9]

A state of society to which such a notice could be perti-
nent would be strange indeed, on first experience, to an
English family accustomed to worship in North Baddesley Church of Hampshire. Other recorded items on
the town book bespeak a world as insulated from the settlements of Connecticut, even from Boston, as from the
Restoration world of London. Who in our town cut or
defaced a tree? Who used false weights or failed to put
the "four bushels of malt per hogshead in the beer?"
Who tied his horse either "*within* side or *without* side"
the fence by the meetinghouse gate? Perhaps a good
world for a boy to grow up in. Certainly one in which to
learn far more than the schoolroom taught, and to remember it for life.

Samuel Sewall had become only a visitor in Newbury
before his father built his second house. It stood on a
portion of the original forty acres he had bought, near

"Trayneing Green," and only a few rods from the schoolroom house of Thomas Parker. To this home the many later visits of the Boston days were made. Son Samuel would continue to come until he was himself past travelling. He would return for the funeral of his father in 1700 and of his mother seven months later. Both lie here in Newbury churchyard. Years later he would write the most nearly poetic passage in all his thousands of pages about this region he first knew as "a poor little School-boy of Nine years and ¼ old." The passage, known to many, appears at the end of his 1697 publication, *Phaenomena quaedam ad Aspectum Novi Orbis configurata.*[10]

THREE

Harvard College

THERE had never been the slightest figment of doubt about his going to Harvard. Accordingly, aged fifteen, the usual time for a well prepared applicant, he arrived. His own word for it,

"In the year 1667 my father brought me to be admitted, by which means I heard Richard Mather of Dorchester preach Mr. Wilson's Funeral Sermon, 'Your Fathers where are they?' " [1]

A more solemn question for the surviving first generation remnant, one might think, than for a fifteen-year-old boy about to begin an independent life for himself, but at the time Samuel wrote this sentence he had remembered not only the fact but the text of the sermon for fifty-three years. Six years in frontier New England with a first generation preacher-scholar as his tutor had given him a sermon ear for life. Also for life he would keep the schoolroom requirement of sermon notes on a page as well as in his memory for Monday morning presentation. In witness whereof his bulky Commonplace books and the many hundreds of sermon items on his *Diary* pages. Sunday sermons and Thursday lectures were fixed engagements in his calendar, and nothing but illness ever left his pew vacant at the ringing of the bell or the sounding of the "kunk" if on a far village journey.

On this important day of August, 1667, father and son had probably ridden up from Newbury on horseback in full readiness. But even with the fortification of Thomas Parker's training consciously behind him, fifteen-year-old Samuel may well have felt some qualms as he stood before the Rev. Mr. Charles Chauncy, President of the college, for his brief oral examination. Could he "read and understand Tully Virgil or any such ordinary Classical Authors," and could he "readily make, speake or write true Latin in prose?" Had he "skill in making Verse?" Was he "competently grounded in the Greeke Language so to be able to Construe and Grammatically to resolve ordinary Greeke, as in the Greeke Testament, Isocrates, and minor poets, or such like?" Such were the first steps in the Harvard *sine qua non* for acceptance. The tests were applied; apparently the proofs were adequate. "Testimony of his towardlinesse" had been met and he was approved. The first hurdle toward a gentleman's education had been safely cleared. He was "capable of his admission into the Colledge." [2]

The next step was to "procure for himselfe a true Coppy of the Lawes of the College" and to copy it for himself. This sheet when signed by the President and by one of the Fellowes was his certificate of admission. Not so easy a routine perhaps as it looks to later eyes, but a fifteen-year-old triumph once it had been accomplished. Years later, when he was managing the Boston printing press, Samuel Sewall remembered this last detail in the matriculation process and suggested that the college *Lawes* be printed and a copy given to entering students, for their greater convenience.

As an entering Freshman in 1667, he probably missed
the usual humiliations suffered during these early years
by Harvard entrants, in imitation of practices in the
English universities, for in that same year, 1667, the
Overseers had ordered that "all such Abuses in that kind
be severely punished by imposing a penalty . . . or by
corporal punishment, as the Corporation shall see fit."
The fact that this formal order was not on the books
until 1674, however, left room for plentiful evasion by
upper classmen, and though "salting" and "tucking"
were already not countenanced, one may surmise that
surreptitiously at least, Samuel Sewall drank the salted
beer, spoke impromptu nonsense from the high table,
and probably had his chin scraped by a Senior thumb-
nail. If so, this was part of the expectation, and he would
have felt deprived to miss it. The most annoying Harvard custom in the Overseers' thought was fagging, or
the incessant errand running and other menial duties
imposed on Freshmen by Seniors, but in spite of this
order, it is likely that Freshman Sewall served his turn
under such bondage. The strictness of the day's program
in college duties might even have made such personal
chores a relief, as free moments from study were rare
indeed. Morning prayers at sunrise or a penny fine for
absence, a pot of beer and a hunk of bread for morning
"bever," classes at 8:00, 9:00 and 10:00 o'clock, "dinner" at 11:00, classes again at 2:00, 3:00 and 4:00, afternoon "bever" at 5:00, "supper" at 7:30, all boys in their
rooms at 9:00 and lights out at 11:00. Such was the
Harvard regimen for the day.

His quarters would have been in the Long Chamber
of the original college building, usually referred to as
Old College.[3] It was the most ambitious building in
New England at that date, still commodious enough

for the small student body and sturdy enough not to worry the Corporation over continual need for repair, as in the next decade. The Long Chamber, which except for the Library ran the whole length of the building on the second floor, provided space for some twelve or fourteen students, and with trundle beds added, could take care of half as many more. Two years later Sewall had Edward Taylor as "chum and bedfellow," but as an entering Freshman he probably had only trundle-bed accommodation. His furniture would have been a wooden chest with a lock for clothing, books and all private possessions; possibly a stool, if he could find one vacant. In addition, in his Sophomore year he would have rented a study, a tiny, closetlike room partitioned off from the Long Chamber, equipped with a shelf, a tableleaf for writing, and a stool. Winter heat except for the fireplace in the Long Chamber did not exist, nor would such comfort have been expected. There were several studies that were warmer, one over the kitchen, one with a fire in it over the Low Chamber, and the west study with a fire, but these would not have been for Freshman rental.

At mealtime the entire college sat in the main Hall, their hats on, eating from wooden trenchers. A student in disgrace sat alone, hatless, miserable. The food was meat, bread, dried peas, hasty pudding and apples, and the drink beer, strengthened by Corporation order in 1661. The tuition of most students was to some degree paid in contributions to the food they were eating: calves, turkey, lamb, salt beef, butter, eggs, apples, honey. A boy could be in residence half a year for a small cow or a barrel of salt pork. Tuition was also paid in firewood, tallow, wax, writing paper, buttons, thread, whatever parents might choose to supply from their own store. All New England fathers were farmers to some extent in those days, and their variety of commodity was surprising.

Supper over, thanks for it offered, all students filed out, bound for the Long Chamber upstairs or into their own studies, until "lights out" at eleven.

What might seem to later young generations the most irksome and unwelcome requirement of the college regime was the order that throughout the day, "within the college Precincts," in class or out of it, Latin instead of English was the language for all instruction, recitation or personal conversation. As the Lawes and Liberties of the College had it,

"The Scholars *shall never use their mother tongue*, except that, in public exercises of oratory or such like, they be called to make them in English." [4]

Of course Grammar School boys were already partially trained in obedience to such a requirement, Samuel Sewall among them, and it may be safely assumed that out of the hearing of the ever watchful tutors, the order was on occasion comfortably forgotten.

During his Freshman year all Samuel Sewall's instruction was in President Chauncy's hands, as had previously been true for students in President Dunster's term. According to the Chauncy code, this meant the Greek and Hebrew tongues four days a week, until late in the year when a student might begin logic, according to his "ripeness" in the languages. On Friday it was rhetoric, or speaking and writing with "elegance" and on Saturday, divinity. In the second year, logic would come first, with language exercises continuing; in the third, ethics, and in the fourth, metaphysics would have emphasis. All undergraduates would take part in dis-

putation once a week, except for the two months before
Commencement and for a fortnight after.

For undergraduates there was little or no flexibility
within this program. Days of study and recitation were
long; margins for individual activity narrow. Outside
of class it was a life lived together in almost hourly
companionship. During the three years toward the second degree this association would be somewhat less constant, with opportunity for brief absence, but when a student was present, more responsibility for the undergraduates in residence. A Harvard education extended
through a seven-year stretch of youth. For Samuel
Sewall these seven years confirmed much that had begun
in the six preparatory years with Thomas Parker, and
also established strong new directions for lifelong, if
sporadic, interest in certain limited fields of intellectual
activity.

Harvard tutors were young men. During Sewall's
undergraduate years, there were three: Thomas Graves,
aged thirty, out of college ten years, Solomon Stoddard,
A.B. 1662, aged twenty-four, and Alexander Nowell,
A.B. 1664, only twenty-two, seven years the senior of
his Freshman pupil. Only a slight disparity, but in the
college hierarchy, a gap wide enough for respect and
deference. That is, usually; but there were examples
of what came close to insubordination in the classroom.
In 1671, when Thomas Graves insisted on reading
Magirus on Naturall Physick to his class, the students
rebelled, refused to read the book and in the end not
only escaped reproach to themselves but brought about
the dismissal of Thomas Graves. Edward Taylor, who
reports this incident, adds that Joseph Browne then took
over as tutor, slighted Magirus, and won the respect,
nay the "very hearts" of his class, so that "wee scarce

ever did any thing wi^tout his advice." [5] Samuel Sewall was in his Senior year at this time.

Protests such as this were immature and sometimes mistaken, but they suggest young independence and courage of opinion which properly belong to an education. In terms of the tight program of subjects studied and the concentration of their pursuit, one might think too easily that this early Harvard education was completely bookish. Bookish, yes, as were its English university models, and yet the emphasis upon the forming of individual opinions, defending them under attack, and the stern exercise of memory instead of lavish use of the few books available imposed an intellectual discipline and developed what a boy possessed mentally, as well as gave him a wider basis from which to proceed in his own thinking.

Even in President Dunster's time, there had been encouragement to what was called "the experimental way of acquiring knowledge as to the external world." Freedom did not exist in theology, but elsewhere let one question as he would. Ten years before Samuel Sewall came, the Copernican system has been the subject of an essay by Zechariah Brygden, which he later included in an almanac he compiled. His conclusions were objected to by Master Davenport, who said none the less,

"Let him enjoy his opinion: and I shall rest in what I have learned til more cogent arguments be produced than I have hitherto met with." [6]

In 1664, three years before Sewall came, John Winthrop, Jr. had presented Harvard with a telescope, brought from England, where he had gone to the founding of the Royal Society. His gift had been received with enthusiasm by the three tutors, and "the real experimental way of acquiring knowledge" commended and advocated. Through the years and especially in 1682, when Halley's comet excited interest, there was opportunity for the public to use the telescope. Many who were not enrolled students came to see.

At no time in its history was Harvard a divinity school. It existed from the beginning to give a gentleman's education to those qualified to receive it. "A nursery of knowledge in these deserts and supply for posterity," Thomas Shepard called it. In slightly different phrase, "to advance Learning and perpetuate it to Posterity," was the purpose recorded in *New England's First Fruits*.[7] Educated men among the founders of Massachusetts Bay Colony were deeply conscious that learning might easily be lost in wilderness living, perhaps in their own very near future. Mere survival was almost a desperate risk and they must make provision at once for perpetuating the "learning" they had brought with them. Transmitting it unceasingly was imperative, and not to the few only. The entire population must be exposed to it. Young children must be taught to read and to understand. Young men must be trained to pass on the learning of the ages.

The place of religion in the thought of the earliest settlers made the pulpit the most likely center from which to transmit this learning, in which religion had a prominent place. To this end (in part) colony law made churchgoing compulsory, with the result that at least some acquaintance with the Bible, approved doctrine, and a sense of human history before his own time was part of even the unlettered churchgoer's possession. By no means were all colonial ministers men of such sensitive experience of religious truth as Thomas Shepard, for example, but he would be an exception in any age.

The average village minister had been trained to read the Bible with some awareness of the ancient tongues in which it had been written, and with some skill to interpret its meaning apart from that time. He could use books, and from week to week most ministers went on with their studies. In sequel, and in differing degree from town to town, the pulpit was the newspaper, the town library, the broadcast for farmer folk, indentured servants, as well as for educated laymen who had come in the first migrations and who might have several precious books of their own.

For the second generation of these first-comers, Harvard College was the prideful concern of every New England village or town. In the desperate first years of the 1640's, when there was little food for today and little confidence there would be even so much a month hence, every family in New England capable of doing so contributed a peck of corn for Harvard College. The depth and stability of this concern for "learning" exists in many records, public and private. It should be remembered along with student numbers, when these went no further than two digits. In New England's day of small totals, a little leaven, as always, leavened the whole lump.

During the seven years of Samuel Sewall's residence in Old College, conditions were less straitened than those during the peck-of-corn gifts, but the college itself was in a period of decline. Things would grow steadily worse until 1674, Sewall's last year, when the college building would be closed, all students out of residence, and the future for New England education dark indeed. In 1667, when he entered, decline was barely apparent, although there were significant changes since the earlier years. In comparison with the three preceding decades,

the college was more fully New England in its student
ranks. The more settled conditions in England were
giving English boys the advantages of their own universities and they no longer came. Proportionately there
were also fewer ministers' sons from New England and
more middle-class boys of non-university fathers in attendance. The routine of college life and instruction was
barely changed, but the wider geographic range of student background, with non-ministerial ambitions for
some students, invited a less heavily religious atmosphere. Among Samuel Sewall's eleven classmates, the
fartherest from the earlier patterns was perhaps Isaac
Foster, a mariner's son, who no doubt brought heroic
tales of adventure by sea, such as he himself would experience a few years later when he was captured by
Barbary corsairs. One may be reasonably sure that in the
private sessions glorified by such tales, the prescribed
Latin or Greek for all conversation "within the college precincts" was happily forgotten.

Of these eleven classmates seven became ministers,
including Isaac Foster himself, Samuel Mather, Peter
Thacher, William Adams, Thomas Weld, John Norton
and Edward Taylor. John Bowles had been called to the
Dedham pulpit, but he died before health permitted
him to begin his work.[8] The three who remained outside
were Samuel Sewall, the most eminent member of the
class of 1671, Samuel Phipps, schoolmaster, and Samuel
Danforth, who died aged twenty-four, before his career
was determined. During President Dunster's fourteen
years as Harvard's first president, forty-five out of
seventy-four graduates became ministers. During President Chauncy's seventeen years there were sixty-six out
of one hundred and twenty-two. The lessening proportion would be natural enough, partly as town Grammar

Schools instead of the minister took over the preparation of boys for college entrance, partly also as trade increased and religion took a lesser place as motive in New England life. All eleven of the graduates in Sewall's class had training that would have made them eligible candidates for the ministry, had they chosen to preach. "Learning" was a candidate's chief qualification, the foundation stone of his eligibility. To young Harvard College for these years goes the honor that one building, one "learned divine" as instructor, and one roomful of students living together in an almost complete communal relationship, could put "learning" in such high place and create the demand to "perpetuate it to posterity" through every pulpit in a frontier colony.

Yet "Scholar and Minister" were not assumed to be identical. In Master Jonathan Mitchell's famous "Modell for the Maintaining of Students and fellowes of choice abilities at the College in Cambridge," [9] young scholars were to be at least "hopeful for godliness" whether they became linguists, physicians, antiquarians, teachers, magistrates. New England needed them all, and "God will not give us such men by miracle." Jonathan Mitchell was pleading for fellowships in their support during student days. "Education in this poor country" will be carried on with "difficulty, hardship and selfe-denyall," he wrote. His *Modell* to the General Court was distributed widely, but came to no practical fruitage. Mitchell himself, as a three-year "Fellow" at the college, had received twenty-six pounds from the College Corn, and he knew the blessedness of such help.

When he made his plea, Samuel Sewall was still a pupil in Thomas Parker's school and decline in public

zeal for education had already begun. "Most men of
the Richer sort" were already putting their sons to
"more advantageous Imployments" than the pulpit
could offer, and opposition to a learned ministry had begun to be vocal. It had been strengthened by sympathy
with Anne Hutchinson's protest against men of books
as preachers. Samuel Sewall's entire college career
would lie within this period of lowered vitality in public
interest. When he was at home during a time of illness
in 1671, he wrote back to Daniel Gookin at Cambridge,
"The College Interest, I fear is remissly promoted
here." After a sermon by John Wheelwright in Newbury,

"But if his Auditors be, as some are; the pines on the beach
will give more attention than they." [10]

So far as we know, Samuel Sewall was not keeping a
diary during his undergraduate days, and there are few
hints, except in far reminiscence, of his immediate response to his four years of disciplined study, or of the
three more in pursuit of his second degree. There is
enough evidence, however, in scores of later references,
to indicate that his reading for life, his own purchase of
books, his interest in theological dispute or biblical interpretation, his fondness for Latin verses, classical al-
lusion or quotation with or without due reason, follow
the patterns of his Harvard training. He accepted patterns and apparently felt no urge to investigate toward
changing them. He had no hospitality to change. He extended his views in maturity, but wherever the extension
took him, the Harvard direction is recognizable underneath.

Years later when the first sponsors of Yale College were asking mature Harvard graduates for suggestions, Sewall's replies amounted to pleas

"To do everything as the late Reverend and godly Learned Mr. Charles Chauncy was wont to doe at Cambridge,"

even to Ames' *Medulla Theologiae*

"diligently read in the Latin Tongue, and well studyed by all Schollers educated in the said School." [11]

Very nearly one half of a century had elapsed since Samuel Sewall had been so trained. He had not moved with the times in education, and more than once was troublesome to the Harvard Corporation because of his unqualified insistence that the traditions of his own far time be maintained scrupulously without change. One item of his particular obstinacy was insistence on the President's exposition of the Bible before all the students met in the Hall several times a week, if not daily. So had President Chauncy done and so should it continue to be after him, world without end. The custom had been given up, or at least become infrequent, during President Leverett's time, because by his own statement, it did not work. Few students were "capable of edification by such exercises," Leverett replied, when criticized for abandoning them. Sewall's insistence had created a strained moment at the Overseer's meeting in 1718, forty-four years after he had left Harvard.

He received his first degree in President Chauncy's last year, and his second from President Hoar, also in his last year. Sir Sewall now became in college protocol, Mr. Sewall, a difference as wide as a gulf in Harvard precincts. During his last three years his studies had concerned divinity chiefly, apparently with the thought of entering the pulpit. Each intermediate step had been standard. Each had brought recognition of his ability. On November 5, 1673, he had been chosen, together with Daniel Gookin, as one of the resident Fellowes or Tutors. One *Diary* item records this new duty in the reading of *Heerboord's Physick* to the Senior Sophisters from December 3, 1673, to March 24, 1674. He began with the fourteenth chapter [he wrote], "went to the end and then red it over from the beginning." [12] This is the first item in his extant *Diary*. He was only five or six years older than his student listeners.

In the following year, 1674, he was given a two-year appointment as Keeper of the college library, an office with rather more honor than labor. The Harvard Library was a very precious area. Only the President of the College, the pastor of Cambridge church, and the Library Keeper had keys. Sewall's duty was to sweep the room, keep the books clean, and to have charge of all records. Books might be taken out at 11:00 A.M. and 1:00 P.M., but only a Senior among students could borrow them. The Library did not exist for undergraduates. Sewall kept this honored post for only a few months, from March to December, 1674, when the decline of the college made it almost an empty assignment.

His M.A. thesis was theological, as were most subjects chosen at that date. Over the years one finds problems in philosophy, law, ethics, church ministry, physiology and medicine, science, biblical interpretation, but theology tops all these in actual choice. Not surprisingly, since instruction throughout the college years had given it special emphasis. Samuel Sewall's title was *An Peccatum Originale sit & Peccatum & Poena*, or freely translated, Is original sin both sin and punishment? He took the affirmative and performed first of the four candidates. As he did not know until months afterward, much of his future was being decided at this public performance, for one fair listener in that august company set her heart upon him in that hour.

In this year 1674, dark months were ahead for Harvard. Leonard Hoar's three years as President had begun in promising new life, but were ending in personal tragedy for him and in deep fears for Harvard's future. He was the first alumnus of the college to be named its head and much had been expected of him. After taking his M.A. in 1653 he had spent seven years in England, been ejected for non-conformity, and returned to Boston under invitation to become minister at Old South Church. Somewhat against his own wish he had allowed himself to be elected Harvard's third president in 1672. He had ideas as to the enrichment of the college life both within and without the lecture hall; a chemical laboratory, a garden and orchard for students "addicted to planting," more recreational life, more specific training toward not only "formal but real scholarship."

Perhaps he proclaimed such innovations too suddenly. Perhaps he lacked the administrative energy and tact to bring them to pass. Perhaps, as some have supposed, he was the victim of jealousy. Why bring a President from England when a likely candidate might be found only three miles away? Whatever the obscure causes of his failure, the effects on the college were ominous for a time. There were only four graduates in 1673, three in 1674, and only three students left in residence. The printing press was unused, the Indian College (never a feasible plan) was deserted, the new Hall left framed only, Old College closed, and all buildings were in need of repair. Dissatisfaction became vocal. The General Court held a hearing on the situation, and charged

Leonard Hoar as "the only burden of the college welfare." He resigned March 15, 1674/75, and died on November 28, eight months later.[13] At the Commencement the following summer Urian Oakes, whose ambition to become President was no secret at this time, spoke truth when he said

"Sad was the house of Harvard, silent was Cambridge, stilled were the studies of all good Arts."

During the General Court hearing on October 13, 1674, as to the causes for the decline of the college, Samuel Sewall had been called to testify. "The sum of my Speech [he wrote in his *Diary*] was that the causes of the lownes of the Colledge were external as well as internal." [14] Such a "sum" of course tells nothing. The word of John Hull, which requires some discount perhaps as the word of a relative, was "Would those that accused him but countenanced and encouraged him with his work, he would have proved the best president that ever yet the college had." [15] Without fuller knowledge this dark chapter still remains something of a puzzle. Undoubtedly this darkness contributed to the bewilderment of Samuel Sewall as his seven years at Harvard came to an end. He had not yet found his place or made a plan for his own future.

One remembers also that in 1674 the Indian war was causing daily terror even in relatively safe Boston, and that King Philip's death on Mount Hope was still months away. There is no indication that active soldiering came into Sewall's mind at this time or later. He was an officer of the Boston Artillery Company for many years, but he was never on a battle field. His education had been preparing him for the ministry since the day he landed from the *Prudent Mary* in 1661, and the logical next step was an offer. It came, as he noted in his *Diary* on November, 24, 1674,[16] from Woodbridge, New Jersey. A letter to his father invited him to become a candidate. He made no comment, but apparently did not consider accepting the offer. Whether from indecision, or from new impulses stirring him otherwise, there is no knowing. But he waited.

FOUR

New Directions

I<small>N TERMS</small> of business success ahead, the prestige of wealth, public office, and doubtless a great deal more (not forgetting a marriageable daughter), John Hull was the most important man in Samuel Sewall's young life at this uncertain time, when long-range decisions were being made. Without him and the doors he opened, there might have been no equivalent to the Mansion House on Washington Street, no entrée to Boston officialdom and no merchandising career, along with higher social and financial standing for a young man from Newbury. Samuel Sewall might very probably have stepped from his Harvard M.A. into the pulpit, served a frontier settlement at Woodbridge, New Jersey, or one like it, and in the story of his generation remained anonymous. Perhaps it was the bustle of Boston as compared with quieter Cambridge, colony officials coming and going, men of affairs on the streets, merchants talking of ships and cargoes, practical concerns instead of the "Tongues," but chiefly it would seem to be John Hull himself, who provided the spur toward a new life.

He had come with his father, Robert Hull, a London merchant, in 1635, and become a Boston resident,

aged ten. This was the same year in which Henry
Sewall, Samuel's father, had arrived in Newbury with
cattle and provisions for making a new settlement.
Robert Hull had bought for his family home a house
standing impressively in a large lot on what is now
Washington Street, near Temple Place and the site of
the present Jordan Marsh department store. When
John Hull was twenty-two, the house became his by gift
of his father. He enlarged it, bought additional lots
adjoining the original site, planted trees, laid out gar-
dens, giving it the dignity and beauty of Mansion
House, as it was called thereafter.

In the following year he made a fortunate marriage
to Judith Quincy, daughter of Edmund Quincy, founder
of the Quincy family in America. Wealth and the connection with the Quincys put John Hull high in the
Boston list socially as well as financially. When the Old
South was founded in 1669, he was one of the founders.
He was a pious young merchant, marked for success,
and as he grew older, piety and prosperity ran strong
and equal in his story. Aging John Wilson is said to have
remarked of him, "God will certainly bless that young
man; John Hull will grow rich, and live to do God good
service in his generation." He fulfilled the prophecy.
His piety was of the traditional first generation quality.
He was not only a church member with clear-cut reasons
for the faith that was in him; he could translate godliness into business integrity. He had also the Puritan
sense of obligation to keep others in line with his own
religious practice, as in a letter to John Harriss, master
of the ketch *Seaflower:* "Wee desire you to let the Lord
be worshiped dayly in yor shipp his Saboaths to bee
sanctyfide all sin & profanes to bee suppressed that the
lords presence may bee with you & his blessing bee upon

you." [1] An ideal, not perhaps an expected fact, but he pressed it.

His business interests were wide. Trained as a gold- and silver-smith, he was the logical choice as mintmaster for the colony in 1652, when money had become scarce, barter clumsy, and abundance of counterfeit coin in circulation. Accordingly, the colony decided to manufacture its own medium of exchange for home use. Ample South American silver was flowing in from trade with the West Indies, why not use it? "They made choice of me for that employment," Hull wrote. He began to coin two-, three,- and six-cent pieces, and best known of all, the willow, oak and pine tree shillings. [2] His mint-house stood on his own family lot, thus bringing industry early to this continuing business center of Boston.

A pleasant royal anecdote attaches to the pine tree shilling record. Whether fact or tradition, the story goes that King Charles II on one occasion expressed indignation to Sir William Temple at the boldness of Massachusetts colony in daring to make her own coinage. "What means this symbol?" he demanded, as he turned the tiny coin in his hand. "Why," answered the quick-witted Sir William, "it is a tribute to your Majesty. 'Tis the royal oak of your famous rescue." Flattered that New England remembered his day in the oak tree, the King cooled his wrath and pine tree shillings continued to be minted in full quantity. [3] John Hull grew rich in the process. He had been business-minded enough at the outset to exact one shilling in payment for each twenty that he coined, and by this arrangement grew richer than he had thought likely. Asked to revise his bargain, he refused and grew still richer, as shillings continued to be minted in still larger demand. When the edges of the coin began to show hacking for the metal that

might be detached, he changed the die, providing a
double rim which made hacking less easy and less profitable. This change also added to the pleasantness of the
design.

In addition to his service as mintmaster, he bought
large tracts of land from which he added materially to
his wealth. Among these were extensive timber lands
near Salmon Falls, Maine, from which he shipped
masts and lumber to England. He acquired, with five
others, the Pettaquamsett Purchase, a large acreage in
the Narrangansett country, including Point Judith,
named for his wife, Judith Quincy. On these lands he
raised horses for export, built and operated a mill. In
Rhode Island he found what he called black lead, a coal
deposit for export to England and Holland. For the
variety and magnitude of his shipments back and forth
across the Atlantic and in the South Seas, he was one of
the principal New England merchants of his time, and
perhaps the greatest of them all for his generation. He
was owner, or part owner, of fourteen ships. The commodities he shipped can be counted by the score, furs,
pipe staves, whalebone, spermaceti, biscuits, butter; the
list is impressive. His imports are significant mainly in
that they included articles for American manufacture
thus early. There were hides for shoes and clothing,
salvaged iron to be made into pots and kettles for home
use. Energy, prudence, and a gift for imaginative ad-
venturing in new directions, for which his inventiveness
and abundant courage would be equal, were fundamental in his nature. In godliness he was, on first sight,
"a right New England man" after the pattern of the
earliest generation.

Like all merchants of his day he took heavy losses
from Dutch and Spanish briganteens, pirates, storms

which would have ruined a man with fewer ventures afloat at the same time. When in 1653 he lost three ships bound for London through Dutch manoeuvres, and one taken by a Spaniard, he wrote, "The Lord wean my heart from these outward things, and fix it more upon himself. The loss will then be gain." He meant what he prayed. When ships arrived safely in England, "The Lord make me truly thankful," he wrote. Once after a loss of £640, "God mixeth his mercies and chastisements, that we may neither be tempted to faint or to despise." He did neither. "God ordereth it so" was a conviction in his thought, as well as on his *Diary* page. God had brought him to a good land, he said, and placed him under choice means. Therefore, "The loss of my estate will be nothing, if the Lord please to join my soul nearer to himself, and loose it more from creature comfort, my loss will be repaired with advantage." [4]

In his own genius, as it would seem to be, for advantage (a very frequent word with him), he was moving away from the Puritan and toward what we call so commonly the Yankee. His record, entitled "Passages of God's Providence," however, gives frequent evidence that he tried to deserve the good fortune that was his, a good fortune that was very important to him. In everything he conceived religion to ask of him, he was scrupulous. On one occasion when he had gone to Medfield to lay out a farm of three hundred acres, his horse strayed, and when he could not be caught, "We were forced to lie in the woods that night." The next day also he could not find him, "and so was forced to come home without him." On foot? Of course. "Else I could not be home before the Sabbath." [5]

A fast at his house, a day of humiliation "for the state of our country," a private prayer meeting, these obligations always had priority. Anyone in need of help: sick, destitute, bereaved, found him waiting; no one went empty away. During King Philip's War he was treasurer of the colony and he used his own money for colony needs when the colony supply was exhausted. At his death £4,000 were owed to him of which only £545 were recovered, and of this sum £400 went for interest, as he had been obliged to borrow the amount he supplied. Such was John Hull.

But put him beside John Winthrop and at once an unmistakable difference is seen taking place in New Englanders of the second generation. It is the sense of having been chosen of God to do a great work that is missing. There is no counterpart in John Hull's busy living to John Winthrop's compelling motive of setting God's city on a hill for all men to see what God had wrought. Religion was not John Hull's way of life. Merchandising was his way of life. Among merchants, he was a godly example, shrewd in business, making money, righteous to the inch mark. Rectitude was without sternness, but still rectitude. Fifty years of frontier life had softened many edges and hardened others. They would be softened, and also hardened, still more for Samuel Sewall.

How did he come to know this man? Naturally enough, no doubt. The beginnings of the acquaintance are not known, but they need present no mystery. Leonard Hoar was John Hull's cousin, and after his arrival from England, he had lived at Mansion House before taking over the presidency of Harvard. As a Fellow of the college and later its Library Keeper, Samuel Sewall's acquaintance with John Hull, in the small world of Boston and Cambridge, was inevitable. When he took his second degree in 1674, it was Hannah Hull, the only daughter of John Hull, who as the guest of the

Hoars in Cambridge had attended the Commencement. She was much impressed with the performance of the comely man on the platform, arguing about original sin, and "set her affection" upon him from that hour. Samuel Sewall learned this pleasant verdict only after he had been married to her for a year and a half.[6]

The marriage was performed in the Great Hall of the Hull home on February 28, 1675/76 by aging Governor Bradstreet, Winthrop's companion on the flagship, the *Arbella* in 1630. At this date Samuel Sewall was twenty-three and Hannah Hull was eighteen. There is perhaps no reason to doubt overmuch the pleasant story of Hannah's weight in pine tree shillings as the measure of her dowry. Even if it be a scrap of folklore, the tale is worthy of our gratitude to Nathaniel Hawthorne for preserving it in his *Grandfather's Chair*[7] to the delight of later generations. Besides, it may be true. Samuel Sewall's ledger entry of 10,000 shillings as the dowry would mean only 1,500 ounces or about 125 pounds, which would seem a reasonable weight for the bride. Hawthorne's suggested picture of the shining new coins poured into one side of the scales to balance her figure in bridal array is a pleasing item in wedding story. Sewall's ledger item reads,

Dr.
Father-in-law, Mr. John Hull, to his Free Promise £500.00.0

Cr.

Feb. 11, 1675   By money received   30.00.0
Mar. 13   By money received   35.00.0
By Balance when new Stated Accts. £435.0.0.[8]

In Boston social news, for an unknown young man from Newbury to have carried off a highly desirable Boston heiress was enough to place Samuel Sewall in a new bracket. Henceforth he was on a higher social level, and Boston doors opened to him publicly as well as privately. The Hull mansion house would be home.

Amid these surroundings decisions for life might be shaped differently. He was meeting new conditions, looking down new vistas. As the son-in-law of John Hull, he might naturally be expected to share in the merchandising responsibilities that provided the comfortable fortunes of the Hull household, and perhaps some day to take them over. Even without the expectation, the interest of this bustling new world might itself prove magnetic. In the daily association with John Hull and his busy concern with ships, ship captains, shipbuilders, agents in London and the South Seas, a new vocabulary of activity challenged the "battle of the books" and "tongues" in quiet Old College and the Harvard Library. He could hardly have escaped coming to terms with the new life which led to Dock Square and the weighing of anchors.

His *Diary* for the immediate months after his marriage contains only a few suggestions of interest in the merchant life, none of them determining and none registering either conscious interest or decision. On one occasion four months after his marriage, he reports going "to Mr. Smith to see the maner of the Merchants." On another, the advice of John Reyner of Dover "not to keep overmuch within, but goe among men, that thereby I should advantage myself." A month later there was the visit of "Mr. Dean" who "Advised me to Acquaint myself with Merchants and Invited me (courteously) to their Caballs." Another month later he recorded a visit of "Mr. Torrey" who "spoke with my Father at Mrs. Norton's, told him he would fain have me preach, and not leave off my studies to follow

Merchandize." Sewall immediately attempted to speak
with the Rev. Mr. Torrey himself, "But he went home
when I was at the Warehouse about Wood that Mr.
Elkins brought." There are other items about being
"called to Business at the Warehouse," [9] which might of
course suggest only a son-in-law's share in the chores of
the family enterprise, or possibly the beginnings of an
interest which was both encouraged and opposed. Soon
or late there would need to be a decision.

A letter of John Hull's four years later, written to his
London agent, Daniel Allin, speaks of a consignment of
hats and glasses sold by Samuel Sewall under Hull's
direction.

"He hath sold your hats and some glasses, and as he can
sell the rest, and receive in, so he will render you account,
and make you a return; and I hope with prudence and
faithfulness, for he is both prudent and faithful." [10]

Deserved adjectives, both of them, in the light of the
longer life story.

Perhaps some of the prudence and also Sewall's lifelong frugality in business owed something to Hull's
tutelage, as one recorded episode hints. As the two men
sat before the fire in the Great Hall one evening, Sewall
threw upon the fire a larger log of wood than John
Hull thought "seasonable," whereupon he administered
a rebuke, declaring that "if he would be so foolish, he
should have no confidence in him: for that his mind
would be as unstable as if it were akin to the wind."
Apparently stung by the sudden outburst, Samuel Sewall recorded the incident in Latin and took comfort in
the reading of Psalms 37: 3, 4, 5, the connection being
a little obscure.[11]

Since a full year before his marriage, when he "holp

preach" for his master, Thomas Parker, he had made
no mention of being in the pulpit. His entry on this
occasion, difficult as preaching might have been in the
presence of his aged teacher, then blind and almost
speechless, does not suggest experienced ease. He was
only twenty-three at the time, and in consenting to
stand there he was of course expressing only a natural
courtesy. With his boyhood friends and neighbors, as
well as his parents in the pew, no wonder he felt timid.
"Being afraid to look on the glass, ignorantly and un-
willingly, I stood two hours and a half," he wrote.[12] The
listener in the pew might also have suffered through the
sermon with him.

With the *Diary* entries as a guide during these first
years of life in Boston, we may infer that he was apparently deeply concerned over his own religious state.
Whether unease because of his minor involvement in the
merchant interest, with consequent neglect of study toward the making of sermons was back of this concern
is not revealed. There are no self-reproaches, only what
would seem to be a disproportionate number of private
religious meetings attended and a statement of his own
"exercise of mind" with regard to his "spiritual state."
The private gatherings he attended were formal in that
one member by pre-arrangement "opened" a Scripture
text, which was then discussed by the other members
present. John Hull belonged to one such group, which
in its turn met at the Mansion House. Sewall speaks of
meetings held at his house, presumably by the same
group. His *Diary* entries seldom go beyond a statement
of the text "opened," who prayed, who spoke, and the
number present.

To what extent, if any, a personal religious search was
the motive back of his attendance at nineteen such meet-

ings in the space of a few months before June, 1677, in
addition to the Sunday and Thursday preaching is mere
conjecture. There is only his own repeated word, once
in a letter on the occasion of his joining Old South
Church, "Sir, I have been and am, under great exercise
of mind with regard to my Spiritual Estate." [13] Many
men of affairs, public officials and business men, attended these meetings regularly. The private fast, or
prayer meeting, at the homes of laymen was a fact of
Boston life at the time, and probably had a fraternal as
well as an intellectual and religious interest for those
who gave time to it. Throughout his life Sewall made a
place for such extra meetings, and his attendance at so
many in the beginning of his Boston residence may have
no further significance than that it was part of the newness of life for him.

He confessed troublement also during these months
over choice of a Boston church, and as the time for the
birth of his first child approached, with immediate
baptism involved, necessity for a decision became imperative. The *Diary* attests his anxiety. With John Hull
one of the founders of the Old South, and the nearness
of this church to the Hull–Sewall home, it would seem
a more likely choice than either the first or second
church, but not without what young Samuel Sewall
called "torment lest this Third Church should not be
in God's way in breaking off from the old." "Torment"
is a strong word in this context, and Sewall talks more
like an old man than a young one in using it, but he can
perhaps be understood in the light of the hostility of
the patriarchs among the clergy and lay leaders of the
two earlier congregations. Argument and counter-argu-
ment, attack and counterattack, a door shut in the face
of a revered pastor, friends at war, and the Boston laity

split into two camps make up this story. Sewall's word in retrospect that he had been "of a long time loth to enter into strict Bonds with God," and of his own "unfitness and want of Grace" would seem to owe something to this turmoil in the church body.[14] Surely it was nothing less than turmoil.

He spoke with friends and ministers, read sermons, attended more meetings and suffered alone, but finally "because of my child (then hoped for) its being baptised, I offered myself, and was not refused." A sermon he had come across in "Mr. Morton's study" had pushed him into action. He wrote out the customary statement, forgetting as he says, "to confess what a great Siner I had been," and was received. His first child was born April 2, 1679, and baptised April 8th. "I named him John."[15]

The uncertainty he had suffered and also the importance he attached to the step he had taken is suggested by his being "overwhelmed" when Goodman Walker came in and did not speak of his having joined the church nor wished him well in so doing. Was he deemed unfit? He was so unsettled by this silence that he could "hardly sit down to the Lord's Table." He did so, expecting that before the ordinance was over, God would give him some special sign that he was accepted. None came. He arose from the table "stirred up dreadfully to seek God," and hoping to do better at the next Sacrament. In this entry, longer, more personal, more detailed than usual, almost articulate, one meets Samuel Sewall when he is trying to face himself. He was twenty-five years old, but talks like one much younger. His concept of religion is as simple as a child's. Perhaps he will be struck dead on the moment because of his unbelief. Shall he miss heaven because of it? His confusion was real, and he had suffered, but it was a young confusion and would end. Not without loss, perhaps; he would not often try so earnestly to search out his own inner self. His remark on the death of Thomas Parker would be more usual with him, "The Lord give me grace to follow my dear Master as he followed Christ, that I may at last get to heaven whether he has already gone." [16] To the end of his life, getting to heaven was the goal of his religious thought, as to many Christians, young and old, schooled or unschooled, in his day.

Unfortunately the entry detailing the Lord's Supper experience in 1677 comes just at the end of the first volume of the *Diary*, and is followed by a break of seven years in the personal record. The next volume is lost. How he regained his balance, and became the calm, self-assured layman of his early maturity is a tale untold. It is a tale we should like to have, for it is not his alone. The current idea of religion as a journey to heaven would henceforth be to him a journey measured less by the conquest of inner doubts, and peace through battle than by conduct that fitted the measurements of righteousness according to the traditional code.

In the following year, 1679, he was made a freeman. He appeared in court and took the Oath of Freedom. Increase Mather and Samuel Willard — later to be his pastor — appeared with him. In this year also as he recalled nearly fifty years later, he became one of the eight constables chosen. "This was my first publick Entrance into the Civil Order." [17] He was also severely ill with smallpox and nearly lost his life. The disease struck first in Charlestown, having been brought in, as was believed, by ships from England. According to John Hull's record, eighty of the two hundred contracting it in Charlestown died. In Boston there were a hundred and eighty deaths, among them that of Thomas Thacher, pastor of the Old South, and John Leverett, governor of the colony.

On October 12, 1681, on the death of John Foster, Samuel Sewall was appointed by the General Court to take charge of the Massachusetts printing press, which six years earlier had been purchased by John Foster and moved from Cambridge to Boston. John Foster was a printer and engraver by trade, and his success with the press had made it well enough known in Boston to provide purchasers for the books he printed. He had printed almanacs, Election Day and Artillery sermons, Increase Mather's *History of the Wars with the Indians*, Roger Williams's *George Fox Digg'd out of His Burrows*, Anne Bradstreet's *Several Poems compiled with great Variety of Wit and Learning*, John Eliot's *Harmony of the Gospels*, *The Confession of Faith*, and a timely broadside, "A Brief Rule to guide the Common People how to order themselves in Small Pocks or Measles." The Boston shop stood over against the "Sign of the Dove" between Washington and Tremont streets, not far from the Sewall home.[18]

Upon his appointment Samuel Sewall immediately engaged Samuel Green, a printer from New London, to do the press work, and for the next three years he selected books to be printed and sold them. His selections show an awareness of local interest and some range of subject. Among those he selected were William Brattle's *An Ephemeris of Coelestial Motions, Aspects, Eclipses, &c*, an almanac of unusual interest, as this was the year of Halley's comet, and for reprint, Increase Mather's *Heaven's Alarm to the World*, the comet interpreted ministerially. John Winthrop's telescope at Harvard somewhat increased scientific inquiry into the comet's behavior, but not for the old-school orthodox. To them God was waving a banner. *Pilgrim's Progress* was in Sewall's 1682 list, only three years after its first publication in England, thereby initiating a long period of popularity for John Bunyan in America. Samuel Willard's funeral sermon on John Hull, 1683, entitled "The High Esteem in which God hath the Death of his Saints," was probably his last publication, for upon John Hull's death he immediately petitioned the General Court for release from the management of the press. His petition was granted September 12, 1684. Responsibility for its management had been far less than absorbing to him and had taken very little time. His life would not have absorbing interests. He would live comfortably within a pattern of Sunday and Thursday sermons, official meetings and dinners, "Treats," he called them, attendance at funerals, artillery trainings, Harvard Commencements, many personal calls made and calls received. After a seven-year beginning to his long Boston life, the pattern, on the death of John Hull, was already established beyond change.

John Hull's death on October 1, 1683, marked Sewall's entrance into public life as an elected officeholder, and also the beginning of his independent merchant activity. These were to be main directions of his mature life, the merchandising for a decade and then tapering off, the officeholding until two years before the end of his life. He was now thirty-one years old, far younger than he seems in many of his *Diary* entries. He often talks like a veteran of many years.

John Hull's estate, depleted as it had been by the use of his own money for the country's needs during his service as treasurer of the colony, left his daughter Hannah and his wife Judith wealthy women for their time. It was wealth in large property interests mainly rather than in money. Two thirds of the estate were Hannah's and one third his widow's. Judith Hull continued to live in the Hull–Sewall home until her death in 1695. The settling of the estate fell to Samuel Sewall. In addition to the transfer of the extensive land holdings, there was also the immediate handling of a many-faceted shipping industry to assume. Six months later, on March 14, 1683/84, Samuel Sewall, Hannah, his wife, and Judith Hull appeared personally in Court, with an "Instrument of Settlement," which they acknowledged to be their own "voluntary act and deed." [19] The Court approved, and confirmed the settlement. A new chapter had now begun.

Because of the shift of center during the preceding seven years from pulpit to warehouse, from religion to business, which was not the shift of one Harvard graduate alone, but of a considerable body of young men, educated or not, we should like to know Samuel Sewall's private thoughts and the steps he travelled from one path to the other. From what he had called "torture" over the founding of the Old South Church, he was now the comfortable occupant of his Sunday pew, setting the tune for the psalm-singing, and when the day was over, entering the text and sermon doctrine in his Commonplace book and his *Diary*. He was a layman for life, his personal religious anxieties quieted, his decision made. On Monday he would go forth equally comfortably to the Town-House to confer with the merchants who met daily on the ground floor, thence to the docks and the warehouses.

Barrels of oil and hogsheads of pickled bass, codfish and sturgeon for shipment, tobacco, grain and cedar shingles for export, and a multitude of commodities to be distributed and bargained for with local shopkeepers; this would be his world. Buying and selling brought new points of view, a new shrewdness, new concern for money. We miss the *Diary* for the years 1677 to 1684, when all this would have been new enough for remark in the daily record. After 1684 it was taken for granted. Should the lost *Diary* volume ever be found, it might annotate a process of change, leading to a shift of culture, not in one man's life alone, but in the life of a generation.

It is easy to say Puritan into Yankee as the terms are usually applied, and the phrase is pregnant with deep truth, but the process itself is enigmatical. Sewall was both Puritan and Yankee, without apparent conflict between the two strains in his nature. He would not have recognized that he was either, and of course would not have known the terms. Seventeenth century New Englanders thought of themselves as British, although when they used the phrase "a right New England man" of their older contemporaries, they meant something very different from a Briton, just off the ship. The earlier men had a firmer righteousness, less personal ambition and for different goals. Plans for mere survival of course came before thought of individual success, and if they thought of success at all, it was in group terms, not for themselves personally. We are here to set our city on a hill, and for religion's sake, not our own. Worldly advancement, riches, even physical comfort were not goals of their dearest purpose or hope. Old Testament godliness, strict obedience to the ten commandments, weekdays as well as Sundays, were both the beginning and the end of their thought. We find these ideals expressed in print, not in their own diaries often, but in the extant sermons to which they listened and talked about until the next sermon was preached. There was a forthright, unswerving quality in a "right New England man" which was hardly recognized for what it was until it had become rare enough among the living to be singled out in those who tarried into this later day. Sewall himself used the term often of the first generation men who were slipping out week by week in the 1670's and 1680's. There was precision in what the phrase connoted in his mind.

In 1703, in a letter to Thomas Bridge in West New-Jersey, he quoted from Charles Chauncy's report of Israel Chauncy's death: "We are left very weak in the fall of our Ancient and Honorable. Very few gray Hairs are to be found in the Colony, in Civil or Sacred Improvements: Sure I am there are now none to be found in this County." Samuel Sewall adds, "And the truth is the Circumstances of the Province of Massachusetts, are much the same with those of Connecticut but now mentioned: Our Ancient and Honourable are much thin'd of late. Mr. Stoughton and Mr. Brinsmead are in particular very much miss'd: and other Cedars in our Lebanon are shaking and ready to fall." [20]

"I account it a great Favour of God, that I have been privileg'd with the Acquaintance and Friendship of many of the first Planters in New-England." [21]

Samuel Sewall himself was not "a right New England man" and could never be. His righteousness was made out of first generation elements, but the intensity, even the passion, behind righteousness in these earlier men was not his to comprehend or to emulate. Unfailingly upright he would be, though not sternly so. He would live comfortably with an edge of luxury and accept his good fortune, as this world saw it, as his natural right. As he took over the management of John Hull's extensive land holdings and merchandising business in 1684, the seven earlier years in the recesses of Harvard would grow dimmer, except at Commencement time. The seven years in the Mansion House had put him on the path to the active rather than the contemplative life. He had just missed being a minister, but the decision was made. He belonged to Boston, and henceforth without apparent uncertainty or troublement in his mind he would hear sermons, not preach them.

FIVE

Merchant Adventurer

THE SHIPPING world had changed almost phenome-
nally during Samuel Sewall's twenty-two years of
New England residence. Boston had only begun to be
a market town shortly before he arrived in Newbury,
at the age of nine. During 1664, when he was twelve,
the coming of sixty ships was recorded. Three years later
the figure was "near one hundred sail of ours and
others," and thereafter the number from year to year
increased ever more rapidly. By 1676 Edward Randolph
reported that citizens of Massachusetts colony alone
owned more than two hundred and thirty ships of above
fifty tons burden, and many hundreds of smaller craft.
Samuel Maverick, a visitor, named Boston "the Metra-
polis of New England" and noted that "the Towne is
full of good shopps well furnished with all kinds of
Merchandize and many Artificers, and Trades men of
all sorts." [1] This was presumably about 1660. No resident could have missed the promise this growth of
shipping had been foretokening for a generation.

New England ships had praise in England and Europe for their sturdy endurance and they were in great
demand. By the 1670's New England shipbuilding was
flourishing in proportion, not only in the coast towns of

Boston, Charlestown, Salem, Ipswich, Salisbury, and Portsmouth, but in many inland towns as well. Abundance of timber and cheap labor were the prime requisites and they were plentifully at hand. In general, as was true for trade throughout the seventeenth century, raw materials went out from Boston docks and manufactured goods came back for retail trade, but there were many exceptions from one cargo to another. English ports were mainly London and Bristol, South Seas ports Barbadoes, Bermuda, Jamaica, Tortugas, Antigua, and the Leeward Isles.

Stern check to this merchandising prosperity had come with the Navigation Acts: trade in English owned vessels only, manned by three fourths English crews only, duties and taxes imposed, all threatened an end to colonial profit; but quite the opposite result was true. Contrary to all prediction, during the early 1660's, while England was too busy with the Dutch wars to enforce her regulations, they were not only widely evaded, but New England profited by shipping what Dutch merchants had formerly supplied. In addition, trade with the West Indies mushroomed, greatly increasing the flow of both imports and exports and more than doubling the prosperity. Ships could go twice a year to the South Seas instead of making only one annual voyage to the Mother Country and back again. Increasing demands arose in the South Seas for new merchandise. Catholic countries needed the fish which New England could so abundantly supply. Improved ships, increased flow of goods back and forth to wider markets, and a New England favorable to buying and selling promised Samuel Sewall a far better chance for commercial success than John Hull had ever enjoyed in the pioneer shipping conditions of his day.[2]

Blows fell, however, and rapidly. Sixteen hundred and eighty-four, the year after John Hull's death, was the fateful year in which the charter of Massachusetts Bay Colony was declared forfeit by decree of Chancery, and all liberties vested in it placed directly in the King's hands.[3] Looking backward from that date, one might wonder why anything else could have been expected, but in 1684, the forfeiture seems to have astounded officialdom and citizenry alike. It was as though the repeated warnings of Sir Edward Randolph had never been made. They now took on reality for the first time. There was truth enough in his report of New England intolerance to non-Puritan belief and rules of conduct, and truth twice over in her persistent disobedience to the Laws of Trade, but sixty years of near-freedom to go her own way had established not only her expectancy of such continuance, but also apparent justification for her independence of royal authority in the matter of trade. There had been no custom house. The colonial governor had cleared all vessels, entering or departing, even though such procedure was out of line with the original charter phrase "no laws repugnant to the laws of England." Even after Sir Edward Randolph was appointed royal custom officer in 1679, whenever colonial vessels were seized, colonial juries could still decide in favor of the defendants.

Looking back on these times, one can see clearly enough that New England was becoming separate from the Mother Country in more ways than she was ready to recognize, and that the requirements of her very different life, largely unknown to herself, were creating loyalties that belonged to her side of the ocean. Crisis greatly strengthened and intensified these loyalties, and when announcement came that the precious charter had been vacated, even delivered into the hand of the hated Sir Edward, these loyalties became powerful. New connotations for the very word "British" were already in the making, and the presence of Sir Edward on Boston streets provided a concrete target on which outraged emotion could spend itself.

It was during these months of 1683–1684 that Samuel Sewall's merchandising activities first challenged his powers singly. Deprived of the experienced counsel of John Hull, he took the burden alone. His personal story during this time cannot be written completely. His *Diary*, resuming after the seven-year silence, is almost bare of items concerning his business life. There are, as original business records, only a five-year Business Journal, 1685–1689, and a sheaf of letters to his British agents for a longer period.[4] From these sources the nature and volume of his shipping during these years can be charted, perhaps with fairness. Both records would seem to attest merchant activity which in range and amount belong to one in a distinctly lower bracket than that occupied by John Hull. It was sufficient perhaps to bring a measure of profit, but hardly great wealth, even according to the standard of his day.

The Business Journal enlightens the record with many details. The book itself is of folio size, bound in sheepskin, and apparently in America. It may even have been home bound and sewn. The dateline on several pages is formal: "Boston in New England in the Reign of King James the 2ᵈ. God Save the King." Under it are cargoes "for the proper acc't and risque of Samˡˡ Sewall," and the detailed disbursements of cargo to Boston shopkeepers.

The ships are mainly ketches, as had been true for John Hull's shipping. One recognizes some of the names that appear in Hull's record. There is the sloop *Sea Flower*, ketches *Endeavour, Fidelity, Prosperous,* and *Hopewell,* the shallop *Green Hill,* the briganteen *Robert and John.* The ketch was a small ship, about fifty feet long, with a burden of twenty to eighty tons.

For ships going to the West Indies, cargoes of fish and oil rank first in volume with pork a close second. Whale oil came next, also in large volume. Boston, at this time, was the commercial New England port for whale oil, largely procured from "drift whales" for which a ship always kept close watch. One yearling whale netted as much as twenty-seven barrels, another thirty-seven barrels. In 1687 the oil amounts went as high as two hundred tons. The Crown exacted a tax for whales and attempted also to enforce strict rules for lancing and cutting. During the early eighteenth century this trade in whale oil increased materially with larger boats for pursuit and improvements as to capture, but it had already been a profitable item in John Hull's shipping. There was also an English and European market for "whalebone prisons for high-born ladies."

Exports of fish to the South Seas appear on Samuel Sewall's invoices as quintals of codfish, barrels of mackerel, pickled bass, sturgeon, alewives. The amounts are large, often thirty or forty barrels in one cargo. Tar, shingles, molasses, often cranberries appear in quantity. Returning ships brought back cedar logs, some of which were reshipped to England, and much Spanish iron in square bars to be made into pots, kettles, kitchen utensils for New England housewives. Salt, wine, rum, sugar also came back in every ship and in large quanities.

Exports to England had changed materially after 1660. In the two earlier decades there had been much wheat, corn, and also many furs. John Hull had shipped

quantities of beaver skins, but by Samuel Sewall's merchandising time, these had almost disappeared from the
invoices. In addition to fish, which still went in large
quantities, he shipped turpentine, at one time five barrels, marked S.S., adding in his letter to Edward Hull,
his agent in London, "It stands me in 40^s here of one
who has made a beginning to get some out of our
Pines." [5] This would be an increasingly profitable commodity later.

Returning ships from London and Bristol brought a
large variety of manufactured articles. Cloth of all sorts
ranks highest, usually of the coarsest kind, but not entirely. Lists include both wool and cotton, and of all
grades, calicoes, duffal, kersies, broadcloth, crepe, serge,
linen, damask, dowlace, lutestring. Trimmings came of
all sorts; fringe, hair buttons by the many gross, hats,
haberdashery, needles, a thousand at a time, and also
many pins. Farm implements also rank high: sieve bot-
toms, milk strainers, cod hooks and cod lines, scythes,
bird shot, nails of all sizes and kinds, rub-stones, castors,
wicker fans for fanning corn, madder — a root used in
dyeing. Sewall's orders from England always included
sweetmeats, chocolate, tobacco pipes, combs, sugar (the
best), oranges and English spirits.

Imports from England also usually show large shipments of firearms, gunpowder, glass, paper, books, medi-
cal supplies, precision instruments. In Sewall's time New
England produced very little of all this, too little to
supply her growing demand. Machinery and skill to
handle their own raw materials came slowly and were
sternly discouraged by the Mother Country.

From Samuel Sewall's detailed lists, it is apparent
that his agent in England or the South Seas must be a
responsible man, since the commodities to be sent in

exchange for his cargo of raw materials must often be left, in part at least, to his selection from what was available, and what would be in New England retail demand. His English agent most frequently written to was Edward Hull, a cousin of John Hull, and a haberdasher at the *Hatt in Hand*, London. He also wrote often to John Ive and John Love. He sold on commission for English merchants, only to a very limited degree. In exchange for one shipment of eleven barrels of mackerel, sent for Ann Quincy, his cousin, he specified that the returning cargo must be "Grocer's Sugar, fit to be disposed of to our Shopkeepers, or in what else you may know to be more for my advantage." To Thomas Burbank of Rumsey he wrote that "the Pack of Serges and Stockings" had not sold well after several trials. "Shall do the best I can for you." Those who have looked on the goods "Say they are charged very high." Besides, he added, "Our going into Mourning for public persons is a new thing, and followed but by a very few." [6] Such hints of New England custom are fairly frequent in the extant letters ordering goods from England particularly.

In ordering two or three hundred feet of "Free-stone squar'd" and twenty-eight sheets of lead 14 × 4½ feet, "by the first good ship" he specified "kindly, well-tempered ductile lead, that may endure the Frost and Sun without cracking or warping." To this instruction he added, "Deal with a skillful honest man that may use me well as to the goodness of the Lead; and as to the price." Nearly always there is a final hint of frugality. To this same order for "Free-stone," he added "60 small Blocks of Stone, two feet long, one foot high, one foot upon the head for coins, also sixty Blocks of three foot long, and one foot square. Let them be such stones as will endure the wether. They will serve for Ballast." If they can be bought cheaper elsewhere, do so. Another seldom omitted touch comes in the words, "Let the lead be sound, without flaws so that if I use but some, or none of it, it may be vendible." [7] These materials were for his own new house, then in building. It was a large structure, built on the same site as John Hull's Mansion House, from which the different sections had been removed to other houses in the neighborhood, apparently by purchase.

Of the milk strainers, he wrote, "Be sure that each Bunch contain a Duz., for the party I sold the last to, complains sundry held out but eleven. Let them be good and well bound." Of the long pipes, "the best glazed." In an order for casks, "Let them be of good Iron, and well made." "Sithes for New England. Long sort, strong, flat Backs, narrow Plates, strong Heels, hard mettal'd." He orders six dozen of them, also six dozen of "Rub-stones," twenty dozen of "strong serviceable knives with bone Horn and Wooden hafts; for which please to sell some of my Iron." "One Sugar Loaf of 8 pounds double refin'd, others single, a Cask of the best sweet-meats." [8] The sweetmeats were usually for Sewall consumption, with a few always in his pocket for calls on the aging widows in his list.

In a cargo of "Pickled Bass" to the West Indies, he specified, "it may go in lieu of Salmon. Please to send the effects in good Rum 4 or 5 hogsetts if the mony hold outt." In return for twelve barrels of alewives to Barbadoes to "sell for ready Money," he asked for "good Cotton wool and Melasses." To Edward Hull in London he sends a "Skillet of fine silver, being Mexican pieces melted down, weighing well one hundred ounces." It will be "proper for a goldsmith." The "midling fans" sent are too small for the customer who ordered them.[9]

In 1687 the briganteen *Robert and John* brought him various kinds of cloth, serge, kersey, canvas, bed-linen, cod hooks, wooden and horn combs, two cases of English spirits. The ketch *Fidelity* brought in return for the produce of her cargo to Balboa 125 square bars of iron, cotton and wool, tobacco pipes, spades, shovels, nails in nine different sizes, shot, lead, frying pans, bellows, books — a typical return cargo from Britain. He exported and imported lumber. In 1691 he ordered "Three Thousand of good Boards; clear, sound, an Inch and a quarter cut," to be sent "this fall, or in the Spring by neighbor Flood by any boatman who may land them at Gill's Wharf, or as near the South-end of the Town as may be." He will give ready money for these. They too were obviously intended for his own new house. For another order of boards — one thousand plank, three thousand inch and a quarter boards, and five thousand inch boards — he said, "Let the stuff come as the trees yield it, good and bad together, and it will serve our Turn." [10] In connection with the payment of a legacy, with which he was concerned, he directed that it be paid in thirty-dozen alchemy spoons, forty brass candlesticks of a middle size, the remainder to be half in brass and the other half in pewter. "The biggest kittles" were not to be above twenty or twenty-four gallons and the pewter platter not above eighteen inches. "A convenient number of basons and porengers" were to be added.

Orders for his own family use are sometimes astonishingly large, always explicit, lavish in certain details, and uniformly with emphasis on the best in quality. For an order of 1706 to John Love for eight yards "black flowered Lutestring or Damask" he specified, "Let the flowers be of Herbs or Leaves; not of animals or artificial things." Of the silks in the same order, "Let there be no Silk Grass in any of these Silks, but let them be all Silk," and not more than six shillings a yard. "Let them be thin strong Silk, for Sumer wear." "If Mr. Storke be slow, quicken him by a Letter, and send p[er] the first good Conveyance." [11]

A single order for his wife, October 24, 1693, from Edward Hull, at the *Hatt in Hand*, London, included materials that would have kept her sewing woman and herself busy for a long time. The payment of fifty pounds was to come from a Barbadoes agent in a cargo presumably sent by the same ship to Edward Hull. The details on this list carry many suggestions, not only of interest for the wares themselves, and the costume details that called for them, but also for their hints of the Sewall family standard of expenditure. The list reads,

One p[iece] of good mixt Serge; blew, Orange, and sad Colours.

Two p^s Stuff, one for Children, the other our own wearing.

One p^e Tufted Holland

Two p^s Strip'd fustian

Five pounds of Cloth colourd Silk; five pounds of black, mostly Sewing;

Five pounds of light-coloured ditto; viz. Orange, blew, red, white colours.

One p^e of Ell-wide Muzlin fine and thick.

Six Ells of Holland at Six^s p Ell.

One p^e Garlic Holland ¾ wide.

One p^e Shepard's Holland, or course Bag-Holland.

Half a p^e of Dowlace, fine, yard broad; if at a reasonable price.

Two pair of black silk Gloves, larger in the arm, and longer than them last sent.

Two p^s of fine ¾ Cambrick.

Sixteen Duz. of Hair Coat Buttons.

Two Gross of Silk ditto Smaller.

One p^e of Coulourd Calico.

Two Gross of Silk ditto Smaller.

If you have more Mony in your Hands, send a pattern of good strong Silk for a Jacket, a p^e of Alamode.

Two p^s of checquered Galoon.

If you have not enough, abate.[12]

Family orders such as this went periodically.

Merchandising would not be a lifelong activity for Samuel Sewall. He pursued it with some vigor and apparent interest for ten or twelve years after John Hull's death, but to judge from his extant records after 1693, the volume tapered off and became largely limited to his own personal needs. His duties on the Superior Court bench placed him in a different world and the path to Dock Square was no longer travelled so regularly. He lent money to many during these later years, and to judge from the extant letters to those who waited years to pay, or did not pay at all, he lost large sums at times. He speaks of charging five per cent interest on these loans.

His duties as representative to the General Court also had begun in the year of John Hull's death. His name appears on the roll of the meeting for November 7, 1683. This was his first public office by election. He was successor to John Hull as the Representative from

Westfield, Massachusetts. At this date a Court member
need not be a resident of the town which he represented,
as was required later, a change which Sewall himself
supported. Edward Taylor, his Harvard classmate and
two year bedfellow, was the minister in Westfield, and
his efforts may have been responsible for this first office.
He continued to serve on the General Court until within
two years of his death, when failing health forced his
retirement. A seat in the councils of government apparently suited him better than management of his own
shipping business, which had hardly been a matter of
free choice in the beginning. He was by no means one
of the great figures in Boston trade for the period when
it engaged his thought and time, but rather one of the
several hundred Bostonians who were called by the term
"merchant," never a very precise designation in his day.

He profited by shipping, however, more than in the
wealth it brought him. Political power had first become
a major goal and also a major reward for Boston merchants in the decade of the charter loss.[13] By the time the
new charter was secured in 1691, the number of merchants in the General Court, the Governor's Council,
and on the bench had increased until they were really in
control of the government. The clergy were distinctly in
second place as the directors of colony policy. That
leadership had ended shortly after the Salem witchcraft
trials. Governor Dudley, after his appointment to the
presidency of the Council, before the royal Governor
arrived, discovered how to benefit New England shippers. He was a merchant himself. Governor Andros,
who followed Dudley, discovered how to curb their
profits. The merchants discovered that the choice of
royal officials in the province could make or break their
business success, and that, to the end of their own profits,

the number of merchants in the ruling ranks was a matter of supreme importance. They secured them.

Samuel Sewall was one of these merchants in the General Court, in the Governor's Council, and on the bench. Like his brother merchants, he walked softly before Sir Edward Randolph on occasion, and though merchant advantage was not his reason, admittedly or perhaps consciously, it is highly likely that to some degree it was back of his silence in regard to the early arrogance of royal officers in Boston. He grew bolder and spoke out more openly in his later years, and was entirely in character when very soon after the first English officers had arrived, he was stirred to vigorous opposition over the holding of Church of English worship in the Old South. Judicially minded as he was, or learned how to be, a religious issue, as he conceived it, could always touch his emotions and bring him to firm action at once. Wherever one attempts to analyze the motives from which Samuel Sewall acted, the central core of his thought and action, in fact, of his individuality, will be found to be religion. One may say, perhaps too easily, that it was religion in a limited concept, but it was the bedrock underneath both thought and action. He acted from it without argument or hesitation, and though he did not always win, perhaps he saved his soul by the stoutness and durability of his convictions under attack. As a merchant he, like John Hull, was accounted by his contemporaries, godly.

SIX

'Twas Never So in Boston Before'

T HE COMING of English officials to represent royal control changed many things in Boston life after 1684. They came in numbers, bringing their subordinates and families with them. Houses were in immediate demand. Redcoats stationed at Castle Island could be seen on Boston streets any day, many of them. Customs, games, celebrations half forgotten by Boston older men and women caught the curiosity and presently invited participation by the younger generation. Here was something new. Bonfires flamed from Fort Hill, loud "Huzzas" sounded down Boston streets, challengers dressed in red and white announced duels to be fought, marching through the street attended with Drum and Quarter Staff and with naked swords advanced, "a great rout following." After the duel was fought, the victorious soldier was led in triumph by his mates, with more drums, more drawn swords. There was shouting in the usual quiet streets by night, gunfire from Castle Island, even on Sunday. It was the "rattling of guns" in sermon time that had called forth Samuel Sewall's phrase, "twas never so in Boston before."

In addition to such surface changes, some annoying and some not, other changes, long in the making but unremarked in progress, became suddenly apparent. Boston was different, and the shock of difference forced comparison with earlier days. The spirit, even the letter of Samuel Sewall's remark, was echoed and re-echoed many times. One finds it in funeral sermons for the aged, preached by the aged; in the persistent jeremiads of election sermons, Artillery sermons, even garden variety Sunday morning sermons, preached by ministers of all ages. The pattern crystallized; and anniversary sermons particularly, which had long been laments for a lost righteousness, now became doubly so. New England was told over and over, until she believed it, that her golden age lay far in the past.

Change had not been sudden, only the awareness of it, and as the new changes of the late 1680's were added, decline seemed more all-embracing. Lament became more superlative in proportion. Some thought the loss of the charter was the reason, and they were wrong. October 23, 1684,[1] was a date in history, not cause of the lost Eden.

As to causes, a new country with doors open and ships afloat to reach it was all sufficient. Only a small proportion of those who had come first had been united in purpose to build God's city in the wilderness. The hundreds who followed them through a generation had come to build their own cities, to start over, to prosper in the new land, not to protest forms and ceremonies in worship, sing psalms and hear sermons. God's kingdom in New England, as John Cotton had envisioned it, had been defeated, not by sin and wickedness so much as by sheer numbers. Hundreds of people, educated and uneducated, middling people, indentured servants, men

BOSTON'S FIRST TOWN-HOUSE
1657~1711

Boston's First Town-House, burned 1711

The Old Feather Store, Dock Square, Boston

2 Pet· ʒ ·14·

Dr· Increase Mather; July, 24· 1715·
p· m· Ps· 90·

James, 4· 14· Whereas you knŏ
not what shall be on yᵉ morrow:
for what is your Life, it is but a
vapor wᶜʰ appears for a while, and
vanisheth away.
Doct· Men have but a very little
Time to be in this world.
1· Experience of all Ages confirm
this· Antediluvians liʋ'd a long
time comparativ'ly; yet they
Dyed: Gen· 5· Shortened much
afterward Ps· 90· Tis unaccoun-
table, that for 3000· years since
it should continue so·
2· God has seen good much to con-
culcat this Truth in his Word.
90· 12· our days; not our years·
Job, 10· 20· thy days are few·
Similitudes, vapor, or Smoke· 102
grass, & flowers· 1 Chron· 29· 15
as a shadow — Job, 7· 6· Swifter
than a weaver's Shuttle

A page from one of Samuel Sewall's
Commonplace books

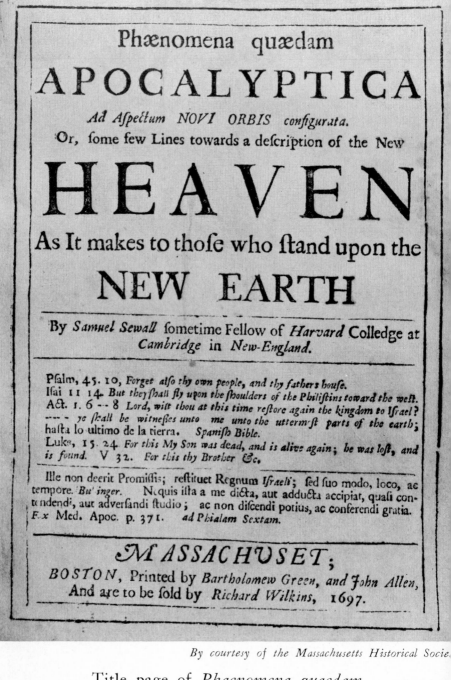

Phænomena quædam

APOCALYPTICA

Ad Aspectum NOVI ORBIS configurata.
Or, some few Lines towards a description of the New

HEAVEN

As It makes to those who stand upon the

NEW EARTH

By *Samuel Sewall* sometime Fellow of *Harvard* Colledge at *Cambridge* in *New-England.*

Psalm, 45. 10, *Forget also thy own people, and thy fathers house.*
Isai 11 14. *But they shall fly upon the shoulders of the Philistins toward the west.*
Act. 1. 6 -- 8 *Lord, wilt thou at this time restore again the kingdom to Israel?* ---- *ye shall be witnesses unto me unto the uttermost parts of the earth;* hasta lo ultimo de la tierra. *Spanish Bible.*
Luke, 15. 24. *For this My Son was dead, and is alive again; he was lost, and is found.* V 32. *For this thy Brother &c,*

Ille non deerit Promissis; restituet Regnum Israeli; sed suo modo, loco, ac tempore. *Bullinger.* Nequis ista a me dicta, aut adducta accipiat, quasi contendendi, aut adversandi studio; ac non discendi potius, ac conferendi gratia. *Ex Med. Apoc. p. 371. ad Phialam Sextam.*

MASSACHVSET;

BOSTON, Printed by *Bartholomew Green,* and *John Allen,* And are to be sold by *Richard Wilkins,* 1697.

Title page of *Phaenomena quaedam Apocalyptica ad Aspectum Novi Orbis configurata, 1697*

The Selling
OF
JOSEPH
A Memorial.

FORASMUCH as *Liberty is in real value next unto Life: None ought to part with it themselves, or deprive others of it, but upon most mature Consideration.*

The Numerousness of Slaves at this day in the Province, and the Uneasiness of them under their Slavery, hath put many upon thinking whether the Foundation of it be firmly and well laid; so as to sustain the Vast Weight that is built upon it. It is most certain that all Men, as they are the Sons of *Adam*, are Coheirs; and have equal Right unto Liberty, and all other outward Comforts of Life. GOD *hath given the Earth [with all its Commodities] unto the Sons of* Adam, Psal 115. 16. *And hath made of One Blood, all Nations of Men, for to dwel on the face of the Earth; and hath determined the Times before appointed, and the bounds of their habitation: That they should seek the Lord. Forasmuch then as we are the Offspring of* GOD &c. Act 17.26,27,29. Now although the Title given by the last ADAM, doth infinitely better Mens Estates, respecting GOD and themselves; and grants them a most beneficial and inviolable Lease under the Broad Seal of Heaven, who were before only Tenants at Will: Yet through the Indulgence of GOD to our First Parents after the Fall, the outward Estate of all and every of their Children, remains the same, as to one another. So that Originally, and Naturally, there is no such thing as Slavery. *Joseph* was rightfully no more a Slave to his Brethren, than they were to him: and they had no more Authority to *Sell* him, than they had to *Slay* him. And if they had no thing to do to Sell him; the *Ishmaelites* bargaining with them, and paying down Twenty pieces of Silver, could not make a Title. Neither could *Potiphar* have any better Interest in him than the *Ishmaelites* had, Gen. 37.20, 27, 28. For he that shall in this case plead *Alteration of Property*, seems to have forfeited a great part of his own claim to Humanity. There is no proportion between Twenty Pieces of Silver, and LIBERTY. The Commodity it self is the Claimer. If *Arabian* Gold be imported in any quantities, most are afraid to meddle with it, though they might have it at easy rates; lest if it should have been wrongfully taken from the Owners, it should kindle a fire to the Consumption of their whole Estate. 'Tis pity there should be more Caution used in buying a Horse, or a little lifeless dust; than there is in purchasing Men and Women: Whenas they are the Offspring of GOD, and their Liberty is,

——— Auro pretiosior Omni.

And seeing GOD hath said, *He that Stealeth a Man and Selleth him, or if he be found in his hand, he shall surely be put to Death.* Exod. 21. 16. This Law being of Everlasting Equity, wherein Man Stealing is ranked amongst the most atrocious of Capital Crimes: What louder Cry can there be made of that Celebrated Warning,

Caveat Emptor!

And

First page of Samuel Sewall's tract,
"The Selling of Joseph," 1700

Suffolk ss.

To the Constables of Boston
or either of them

Whereas I am informed that one Mary
Grigg Gilligen single-woman is now in this Town
great with Child of a Bastard, and is
likely to be chargable. These are therefore in His Maj^s Name to command you forthwith to
bring the said Mary Grigg before me, or
some other of His Maj^s Justices to give
in security that the Town be not charged
and further to doe & receive as to Justice
shall apertain. Hereof you are not to
fail. Given under my Hand and Seal at
Boston this 5th Septr 1700. Annoq; RR^s
Gulielmi Tertij Angliæ &c. Duodecimo.

Sam Sewall.

By courtesy of Goodspeed's Bookshop, Boston

A writ, September 5, 1700, in
Judge Sewall's hand

Lords-day, June, 16. 1700. mr. Daniel
Oliver has his Son Daniel baptiz'd.

Born
Febr. 19th
1653
ӕ
mr
Eyre
Dies.

June, 17. Mr. John Eyre makes his
Will in ye morning, and dies in ye
Afternoon, an hour or 2. before
Sunset. I visited him on Satterday
in ye Afternoon: He was sitting up
in his little Room, took me by ye
hand at first coming in, Desired
me to pray for him when took leave.

Fourth-day, June, 19. 1700. Mr. Jno
Eyre is entombed in the new burying
place. Nine of his children are laid
there, to handsel ye new Tomb:
Bearers Sewall, Addington, Townsend,
Byfield, Dumer, David: Scarvs &
Rings. Lt Govr and many of ye Coun
-col there. Mr. Thomas Brattle led
his mourning widowed Sister. When
I parted, I prayd God to be favourably
present with her, and Comfort her in
ye absence of so near & dear a Relation.

Selling of
Joseph.

Having been long and much dissatisfied with ye Trade of fetching Negros
from Guinea; at last I had a strong
Inclination to write something about
it; but it wore off. At last reading
Bayner Ephes. abt Servants, who men
tions Blackamoors; I began to be un

Pages from Samuel Sewall's *Diary*

Aug. 19th 1692. This day the Lieut Gov
Major Phillips, mr. Russel, Capt. Lynde
& my self went to Watertown. Advis'd
ye Inhabitants at yr Town-Meeting to settle
a Minister; and if could not otherwise
agree, should first have a Town-Meeting
to decide where ye Meetinghouse should
be set: many say Whitney's Hill
would be a convenient place.

This day George Burrough, John
Willard, Jno Procter, Martha Carrier &
George Jacobs were executed at Salem
a very great number of Spectators be-
-ing present. Mr. Cotton Mather was
there, Mr. Sims, Hale, Noyes, Chiever
&c. All of ym said they were innocent,
Carrier & all. Mr. Mather says they all
died by a Righteous Sentence. mr. Bur-
-rough by his Speech, Prayer, protestation of his Innocence, did much move un-
-thinking persons, wch occasions yr speaking
hardly concerning his being Executed.
Augt 25. Fast at ye old church respecting
ye Witchcraft, Drought &c.

Augt. 27. abt 4 p m Cous. Fissenden
comes in & tells ye sad News of Simon
Gates being dead of ye ~~~~~~~~ Fever
died yesterday & is buried to day. I
heard not a word of it, & so neither
saw him sick; nor was at his Burial.

and women without a group purpose, without a plan, but with vague dreams of a new life, had come on every ship. They cleared land, settled towns, raised stock, brought forth children, and now these children were rapidly forgetting what lay behind them. Many memories are only a generation long. By 1684 the secularization of New England life, as compared with the first days, was everywhere: in the home, with the abandonment of morning and evening psalm and prayer; in the church, with the refusal of those desiring to join the membership to appear before the church with written Relations of their previous Christian experience; in the town, with defiance of laws regulating behavior by day and by night. Election sermons decrying change had all the examples at hand any preacher could ask, but the long list of current sins which he asserted had provoked God's anger had a hollow sound to the multitude.

Samuel Sewall indulged in no jeremiads. He was by nature not inclined to look on the world around him with a disapproving eye. New England had been kind to him, and in his comfortable prosperity he lived on an even keel. When his turn came to "watch by night," he went forth with his neighbor Isaac Goose and the others whose turn it was to watch with him until 5:00 A.M., and more often than not, the report turned in would be "Town quiet. All well." Boston to his eyes was not an evil city, though when misdemeanors and crime were uncovered on his night rounds, he could deal with those out of order with the severity tradition demanded. He could also stand by when a criminal was "turned off" at the gallows without a quiver of sympathy. He could refuse to attend the funeral of a "notorious drunkard"; insist that Increase Mather's sermon on the "Horrid Crime of Self-Murder" be republished at once, when a poor boy had taken his own life. Why save his mother's feelings? She was merely trying to "brave it out." Self-murder was a heinous crime; others should be warned. Righteousness, as Samuel Sewall saw it, was on one side of a clear, firm line, sin on the other, and his emotions reversed at the line.

They reversed also, sometimes quite as strongly, at the line between Boston traditions of the earlier days and the substitution of different ways, whether older or not. It may be too kind to call this way of thought and action conservative. It was perhaps too adamant, too unbending, too lacking in imagination, too final for that. What saves it (perhaps a little) is that back of his mental closed doors there was somewhere a Bible verse for which, as he saw it, there was one interpretation and only one. Perhaps conviction is too kind a term also, but look for the Scripture basis for it, and it is always there. Whether the application be of consequence or not was of lesser importance. A rock to tie to was requisite, and for him that rock was the Bible. He used it as a lawyer uses a statute. It was unassailable.

On naming an ancient Massachusetts law as warrant for action on one occasion when illness prevented him from attending the session, he wrote,

"And therefore I am against entring into a way never yet gon in, not beaten, and therefore not likely to be the King's Highway. Innovations are to be suspected, and avoided." [2]

This was a leading principle in all his thinking.

To a man whose thought was governed by this premise, the changes all around him after 1684 promised troubled days. Nor was the troublement less because many of these changes, even at the time, looked too minor for deep concern. To read his *Diary* report of history in the making during 1684–1690 is to be struck again and again by the unawareness of a contemporary record as to the significance of the passing hour. When history writes the story long afterward, major and minor will perhaps change places many times. Yet to lose the sunrise to sunset view in a time of crisis is also a loss to history itself in subtle ways. Any diary is in its very nature the unsorted story of the day as it passes. To read Sewall's record in mere snippets is to lose the persistent overtones and undertones. To read it day by day, month by month, is to find history in it.

During the first shock of this troubling change he was in his second term as representative in the General Court, and as one on the inside, able to supply details not observable to the citizen freemen. Read from day to day for what official records do not supply, his report of official life during these months is the tale of unrest, disunity, rancour, tension, friction, often to the point of harshness. There is frequent "heat between members," a "sudden gust, hardly knew what he said," "extreme sudden and tumultuous" disagreement, sharp words, uncomfortable meetings. The same note comes in his record of the attitudes of the "People" who stood apart from their leaders and were openly critical of them. There is "extreme Displeasure" among them against Joseph Dudley, pro tem president, and his deputy, William Stoughton, appointed until the coming of the royal Governor. Sewall himself reports frequent conferences with both Dudley and Stoughton. They call on him; he calls on them; they dine at his home. Stoughton once came to him by night, as though secretly. Yet there are hints of dissension in these counsels.

As Samuel Sewall reports his own words in the Council meetings, the "People's" charge of apathy toward the new rulers is clear. He is passive, lacking in a fighting spirit, such as he describes for the people, whose indignation he calls "Extream." In April, 1686, when Colonel Shrimpton's remark, "No Government and Company in being in this place," was pronounced "treasonable" and put Shrimpton in prison, Sewall quotes himself as saying, "Am afraid little can or will be done." At the last meeting of the Old Government, when all but four of the Old Guard had gone, "The foundations being destroyed, what can the Righteous do?" [3] He was speaking against a protest such as the people were demanding, and speaking as a realist, but this was the spirit under sharp criticism by the people. An "abusive libel" was found on Dudley's fence one morning, but the decree of Chancery was not changed thereby.

Publicly, however, the people appeared tractable. Ordered to proclaim King James II, thousands swarmed the High Street, drums beat, trumpets sounded, volleys were fired, and loud huzzas responded on all sides. "An Humble Address" sent to the King to assure him of our "great grief and Sorrow wee are fallen under your Majesties Displeasure," but in the *Diary* record "Displeasure" is everywhere. Thirty-one ministers meet to give their opinion as to what the government should do when the Commissioned Governor arrives. "It ought not to give way to another till the General Court had seen and judged of the Commission," said the spokesman, Mr. Hubbard. Not all agree with him. "The meeting has been uncomfortable," Sewall reported, "and I doubt will breed great Animosities." Among the deputies "fierceness in discourse," "very sharp debates" continue about "submission" when the Governor arrives. There is "an Uncomfortable Court Day" by reason of a phrase "the Peace of England" to be inserted in a

Thanksgiving Proclamation, and because of no agreement there will be no Thanksgiving Day. When Colonel
Shrimpton failed to appear for his trial for his "treason-
ous words," as ordered to do, Sewall wrote, "So that this
Monday we begin palpably to dye." [4] To follow through
many pages, as he reports the response to public events,
rumors, announcements, both in Council meetings and
on the street, as all wait for the arrival of the *Rose
Frigot* to replace rumor with fact, is to sense disheartenment and disunity, in leaders and people. New Englanders were not yet Americans. Another hundred years
would forge disheartenment and a sense of futility in
protest into united purpose and action.

Yet in the long record of the *Diary*, these items suggesting adverse public feeling or his own passiveness
under what is happening are almost incidental. The
pages of the *Diary* are full, as always, of ordinations,
sermons, funerals, commencements. Sewall held a fast
at his house to which all the magistrates and their wives
were invited. There was praying and preaching. "Mr
Moodey prayed about an hour and a half. Biscuits, Beer,
Cider, Wine were distributed." Little Hull's convul-
sions grew severe. "He can say Appel." A barn burned.
A porpoise was pursued. When William Adams, one of
Sewall's classmates of Harvard days, was buried, "I took
one spell at carrying him." "An Indian is branded in
Court and a piece of his Ear cut off for Burglary." "Mr.
Eliot's Collar bone is broken near his shoulder which
puts him in great pain." "The Governor's Hat blew off
and fell flat on the Ground just as he went to go in's
Gate." [5] These are standard items in the day's record,
not greatly different except in number and length from
what one might find in an interleaved almanac of these
same days.

On June 20, 1685, he reports, "Carried my Wife to Dorchester to eat Cherries, Raspberries, chiefly to ride and take the Air: The Time my Wife and Mrs. Flint spent in the Orchard, I spent in Mr. Flint's Study, reading Calvin in the Psalms, &c. 45, 68, 24." [6]

On November 12, 1685, "Ministers of this Town Came to the Court and complain against a Dancing Master who seeks to set up here, and hath mixt Dances, and his time of Meeting is Lecture-Day: . . . Mr. Moodey said 'twas not a time for N.E. to dance. Mr. Mather struck at the Root, speaking against mixt Dances." [7]

On Christmas Day, 1685 (which Sewall always called December 25th), "Carts come to Town and Shops were open as is usual. Some somehow observe the day; but are vexed I believe that the Body of the People profane it, and blessed be God no Authority yet to compell them to keep it." [8] Such is the panorama of life as usual, in hundreds of miscellaneous items.

Occasionally there is a page that is history itself. It could not have been written after the day or by anyone not present at the scene. Such is the entry for May 17, 1686, the last meeting of the Old Government, aged Simon Bradstreet, Governor. "General Court Sits at One oclock, I goe thither about 3. The Old Government draws to the North-side, Mr. Addington, Capt. Smith and I sat at the Table, there not being room: Major Dudley the Praesident, Major Pyncheon, Capt. Gedney, Mr. Mason, Randolph, Capt. Winthrop, Mr. Wharton came in on the Left. Mr. Stoughton I left out. Came also Capt [of] King's Frigot, Gov'. Hinckley, Gov'. West and sate on the Bench, and the Room pretty well filled with Spectators in an Instant. Major Dudley made a Speech that was sorry could treat them no longer as

Governour and Company; Produced the Exemplifica-
tion of the Charter's Condemnation, the Commission
under the Broad-Seal of England — both: Letter of the
Lords, Commission of Admiralty, openly exhibiting
them to the People; when had done, Deputy Governour
said, suppos'd they expected not the Court's Answer
now; which the Praesident took up and said they could
not acknowledge them as such, and could no way
capitulate with them, to which I think no Reply." [9]

It was after this ultimatum that Sewall, when only
four of the Old Government were left in the room,
spoke against making a protest. He knew it would avail
nothing. Instead he suggested that on the morrow some
of the Elders be called together to pray, but his suggestion was not accepted.

Four days later, May 21, 1686, the magistrates and
deputies went to the Governor's. They "discoursed,"
said Sewall, about delivering the keys of the fort, as
demanded. After prayer, in which God was thanked "for
our hithertos of Mercy 56 years," Sewall "moved to
sing," as they did, the 17th and 18th "verses of Hab-
akuk." They did not dissolve the Court, but agreement
"to adjourn" until the second Wednesday in October
"was declared by the Weeping Marshal-General. Many
Tears Shed in Prayer and at Parting." [10] A period of
history had ended for Massachusetts colony.

On this same day the *Rose Frigot* "came up with a
fair wind, the Castle fires about 25 Guns, the Sconce and
ships respond, also Noddles Island, Charlestown, Bat-
tery, Frigot again, Ships with their Ancients out, and
Forts and Flaggs." There were few spectators on Fort
Hill, Sewall reported, and "no Body that I observed
went to meet the Praesident at his first coming to Town
that I know of." [11] Always mindful of what official

courtesy demanded, he waited on President Dudley in the morning and accompanied him to town, a politeness that might have been misunderstood by the "Displeased" people.

The first challenge to Samuel Sewall's loyalty to New England tradition came immediately. He knew that it was coming and stiffened his resolve. When he appeared in the Council to take his oath as Captain of the Artillery of the South Company, he went as to a duel. Hear his own word, "I read the Oath myself holding the book in my Left hand, and holding up my Right Hand to Heaven." [12] Perhaps the conviction in his bearing silenced correction, for his New England way of swearing an oath went uncorrected. Swearing as the English magistrate expected called for holding the Bible in both hands or laying hands upon it, and then kissing it, a gesture which to orthodox New Englanders was idolatry. To Samuel Sewall and many others at that date an important issue was involved from this hour, and he took part in the sometimes bitter controversy with untiring spirit. Sometimes an English officer was lenient, but more commonly, refusal to swear the British way meant a fine, and if the fine were not paid, imprisonment resulted. A minor issue to later times surely, but to the conscientious on both sides at this date, held to obdurately. Sewall was by no means in a small minority.

How feeling ran is suggested by the remark of the Rev. Mr. Torrey, who when asked his opinion by Samuel Sewall, replied that he would suffer anything but death rather than lay his hand on the Bible in swearing. Once when an attorney was to be sworn before Sewall, "Mr. Dudley ask'd for a Bible, I ask'd if it might not better be done without. He Laugh'd and seeing a Bible by accident, rose up and took it." [13] To Sewall the laughter was past understanding. A principle was involved, in part religious, and in part, though he did not know it, loyalty to their own custom of long remembrance. But the laughter would win, and a younger generation would not have a long custom to remember or argue about. Still troubled, Sewall went to aged Governor Bradstreet and repeated his question. "He told me," Sewall reported, "that he and some others did so swear [the New England way] on board the ship. And that he never Knew an Oath administered any other way after he came on Shoar." But he added, and something comes through about Governor Bradstreet in his quiet word, "It is all one to touch a Book and swear by a Book." He was not one to strain at a gnat or swallow a camel.[14]

Sewall's punctiliousness over small details is everywhere in his story. Everything to the inch mark, decently and in order. Such scrupulousness being true of him so unfailingly, one is touched by the relaxation of his precision, when years later he visited his aged father in Newbury, two days before his death. After reading the Bible together in the morning they went to prayer. The old man struggled to stand up, but "I persuaded him to sit still in his chair." [15] A nice touch, and in keeping with the gentleness that was also a part of Sewall's nature. Two days later, before his son returned, Henry Sewall was gone. But this was years after 1686, when Samuel Sewall had learned how to learn.

Also immediately after the new Governor's arrival there was the cross in the colors to cause him even greater distress than the method of swearing. His Captain's commission in his pocket, he appeared on the training field, only to discover that his men would march under St. George's cross. He was "in great exercise and afraid if I should have a hand in 't whether it may not hinder my Entrance into the Holy Land." [16] He "seriously discoursed" with his fellow soldiers about it. Most of them were not so much "exercised" and fearful. For military companies this issue had not vexed New England since 1634, when Governor Endicott in anger had cut the offending symbol from the colors with his sword. The peace of the very young colony had been shaken by his boldness, he had been disabled from holding office for a year, and in partial compromise the cross had subsequently been left out of the colors for all military companies, but had flown from Castle Island. After more than fifty years to be obliged to put the hated emblem in again seemed unlawful to those who could remember the furor. To the newer generations it was a novelty, and without more than passing interest. They were wearing paper crosses in their hats when Sewall arrived. He "fetched home the silk" which was to have made the cross and "went and discussed with Mr. Mather."

Cotton Mather judged it sin, but thought the blame would not be upon the wearer. Sewall was not willing to take the risk, and he resigned his commission. A minor issue again, but it cost both of them courage, and for Sewall, sacrifice as well. Nothing in his public service thus far had given him more satisfaction than drilling the South Company on Training Day. One is glad to know that he was later restored to his command.

Only five days after the discovery of the cross in the colors, came another reminder that New England was no longer ordering her own affairs. This was the immediate demand for a Boston meetinghouse in which to hold Church of England services. "Mr. Ratcliff," the minister of the English group, made the request at the first Council meeting and was straightway refused. He was told that instead he might have the use of the East-end of the Town-House where the Deputies used to meet, "until those who desire his Ministry shall provide a fitter place." [17] Worship was deferred for a week until a pulpit could be provided, and thereafter it was "carried up and down the stairs" when a service was to be held. Many crowded into the small room for the first morning and afternoon service, and it was apparent that this makeshift would not last long.

There were few residents in Boston at this date who had ever attended a Church of England service, and there was a keen curiosity over those forms and ceremonies which all their lives they had heard were outrage and pollution. To the strictly orthodox New Englander this exhibition was what "our fathers had fled from" and now it was in our midst. To their New England children the "pollution" was less monstrous than they had imagined, and probably they were disappointed. Truly the wife of Secretary Randolph was seen "to bow at the name of Jesus, even in prayer time," but this was not highly dramatic. Sewall reports this small detail. The congregation at the Old South listened carefully to see whether Samuel Willard prayed for the king or did not. For both English and New English, church ways, even in such minute details, became newly important. There were several Church of England weddings to make conversation, and three Book of Common Prayer funerals before the death of Lady Andros. Samuel Sewall attended her funeral, with all the Council, and reported the candles, torches, the mourning women, and bells. The King's Declaration for Liberty of Conscience had less attention at the time of its announcement than these unfamiliar details of English worship.

The meaning of the Declaration became clearer when the East-end of the Town-House became too small, spelling trouble for the orthodox. Immediately after the arrival of Governor Andros in December, the procession to the Town-house, Guards of all eight Companies attending, and the administration of Oaths (the Governor keeping his hat on, as Sewall reported), he spoke to the ministers about the accommodation of a meetinghouse in which church services might be held, to the convenience of the Boston congregation and his own. A natural request surely, and one which one might assume would be met not only graciously but gladly, but not in New England in 1686. On the following day the ministers met with four members from each of the three congregations and agreed (in Sewall's *Diary* record) that they "could not with a good conscience consent that our Meeting-houses should be made use of for Common Prayer Worship." This answer was taken to Governor Andros by Increase Mather and Samuel Willard. All seemed to be quiet until March 23rd when Governor Andros sent Edward Randolph for the keys to the Old South "that may say Prayers there."

Samuel Sewall was one of the six men who waited on "his Excellency" "to show that the Land and House is ours, and that we can't consent to part with it to such use." [18] They took with them an abstract of "Mrs. Norton's Deed" and explained how the building "was built by particular persons, as Hull, Oliver, £100 apiece." It is "our Meetinghouse." Two days later the Governor ordered the sexton to ring the bell and open the door. At the Governor's command he obeyed, although ordered differently by the Old South, and Church of England services were held.

The consternation, dismay and indignation of the Old South were extravagant. To take "our Meetinghouse by Authority" was an affront. Use of it for a ritualistic service was a pollution. But protest was un-availing. Services both regular and special were held there henceforth every Sunday. Arrangements were worked out with difficulty so that both congregations could be accommodated, but the hours agreed upon were not kept and resentment flamed. The Church of England service was to come first. On March 27th "the Governor and his retinue" arrived at eleven o'clock but the service "broke off half past two because of the Sacrament & Mr. Clarke's long sermon." Meanwhile the street had been crowded for an hour with the Old South congregation, standing irate in the chill March wind. It was by such incidents, minor but not trivial, that New England through long weeks to follow learned the meaning of the new royal government, "in a Scarlet Coat laced," as the Governor was escorted back and forth in Boston streets by attendants also in scarlet.

The more orthodox of the Old South congregation attempted through the usurpation and broken Sunday peace to keep their consciences clear by extra meetings of their own. Samuel Sewall held a private fast at his home on June 1st, to atone for the "putting off of the Sacrament the last Turn, and the difficult circumstances our Church is in above others, regarding the Church of England's meeting in it." [19] Two sermons were preached on this private occasion, one by Samuel Willard, and one by Cotton Mather. Irregularity was distressing to Samuel Sewall and he also felt a sense of guilt, which one hopes was relieved by this extra sermon. There is no rancour in his account of the need for an atoning service.

On another Sacrament day when the Old South service lasted fifteen minutes over the twelve o'clock deadline, Governor Andros was angry, as he took his turn at standing in the street. He retaliated by causing an hour and a half delay for the Old South afternoon service on the same day. A few days later when Sewall and Captain Frary waited on the Governor in protest for this altering of the meeting time, a stormy session ensued. His Excellency asked "who this House belonged to?" "We told him the Title to the House was on Record." [20] This retort accents the Massachusetts resentment to the Crown's claim to all land titles, by all odds the principal source of uneasiness throughout the entire Andros regime and in the whole colony. The Governor's question on this occasion was being answered daily as landholders were told their titles were worthless. Land not bought under the Royal Seal was still the property of the Crown by right of discovery. Indians had a right to live on the land but not to sell it, and their deeds to New England towns under their mark were null and void.

Samuel Sewall's extensive land holdings made his fears large in proportion and he was deeply worried. These fears were quickened when on March 28, 1688, he was approached by Church of England adherents in Boston and urged to sell them a piece of his Cotton Hill property for the erection of a Church of England building. Interviewed by Captain Davis, he reported his answer. "I told him I could not, would not, put Mr. Cotton's land to such an use, and besides, it was Entail'd." On a second urging by Edward Randolph, he repeated his refusal. "I told him I could not, would not, set up that which the People of N.E. came over to avoid: 2ᵈ The Land was Entail'd." [21]

His suspicions as to what might follow were borne out when on July 12th he learned "There is a Writt out against me for Hog-Island, and against several other persons for Land, as being violent intruders into the King's possession." [22] Hogg Island included four hundred and ninety-eight acres of Sewall's land, dearer to him than any other of his many land holdings, and he immediately set about it to secure the title, costly as he knew it would be by application for a royal patent. His efforts would also involve a trip to England before the year was over.

A week after learning of the writ he petitioned for a royal grant and confirmation of the title "forever under the Seal of this his Majesties Territory upon such moderat Quit-Rent as your Excellency shall please to order." It was not a moderate quit-rent apparently, and as he found out later, only a few of the wealthier land-holders, Dudley, Stoughton, and other "principal men," had been served with the writ, frightening them into paying the high price demanded. Immediately Sewall bought other sections of the island not included in his original deed. On October 2nd he went with Thomas Newgate, a Boston lawyer, "in the rain" and "under a canvas covering" took "Liberty and seisin" of Joseph Sowle's marsh. This ceremony was according to English law. There were four witnesses, he wrote, "only one of whom could write his name," [23] a hint of the lapse in the education of rural community children all over New England at this time.

He was much criticised by the "People" for acceding to the British demands in this method of purchase and also for petitioning for a royal patent. "They look on me very sorrowfully that I have given way," he wrote to Increase Mather in London.[24] In this same letter he inquired urgently whether "persons are thus to be compelled to take out Patents." He also told Increase Mather that he had expected to come to London in the ship which would bring this letter, but his friends would by no means "part with me, my wife being near her time."

SEVEN

The English Journey

ON SEPTEMBER 17, 1688, he noted in his *Diary*, "I speak to Mr. Gillam for a passage in his Ship." The journey to England was personal, not official. Its most urgent purpose was confirmation of his rights to Hogg Island and his other New England properties, if possible without the heavy charge for the English patent already applied for. He also wished to attend to his father's and his own properties in England, to meet his shipping agents and, somewhat vaguely in purpose, be of whatever help he might be to Increase Mather in his plea for restoration of the lost charter privileges. In addition, he wrote, he wanted "to see my native country, while some that I know are there." [1]

He had been away for twenty-seven years, and though such knowledge as he possessed, in addition to his own small boy memories, had come only through his father and the frequent family letters from Hampshire, he still had a strong sense of his British origin. This English journey, although it would strengthen that sense, would also make him more completely a New Englander than ever before, and with new satisfactions in being one, as was true for others who returned to New England after

brief intervals in the Mother Country. He was now
thirty-six years old and would be absent for an entire
year.

Leaving Boston meant delays. Local action on his
Hogg Island petition was still pending, and since it had
been presented to the Governor on July 24th, he hoped
to hear before he sailed. His wife Hannah was expecting
the birth of another child. For a man of his temperament
and way of life, there were also all but innumerable
visits and calls to make, consultations with his friends
over details of the voyage, a day of private prayer (for
the journey) at his house, dinners public and private,
even stones to lay and nails to drive in meetinghouses
and private houses under construction before he could go
with a clear mind. A man of office in Boston did not slip
away quietly on a private journey in 1688. At least
Samuel Sewall did not. On August 15th the child was
born, Son Joseph, baptized the following Sunday, and
named for "the first of that name," as his father wrote,
"in hopes of the accomplishment of the Prophecy, Ezek.
37th, and such like." [2] This son was destined, grown
man, to be his father's pride and joy in a long pastorate
at the Old South. At this date Samuel Sewall had lost
four sons; John, his first born, Hull, who had lived two
years, Henry, only two weeks, and Stephen, six months.
There were now only Samuel, aged ten, and two daughters, Hannah and Elizabeth, in the home. On Wednesday, October 3rd, there was a private prayer and preaching meeting at the Mansion House, with Samuel Willard as the preacher. After the service of prayer and
psalm-singing which followed, fifteen had sat down to
the table.

All this took time, until on October 10, advance
preparations being nearly over, Samuel Sewall went on

board Captain Clark's ship, was introduced by one of the owners, and "took up the Starboard Cabbin." On October 15th he arranged to have a barrel of beer bottled for his own use on the voyage. On board were "Two Canvas Baggs, one qt 675½ Ounces of fine Silver in 3 Pieces — 125 ½ English Coin — 7 ounces gold dust," shipped to himself on the *America* to his English agent. This would pay his expenses on the trip.[3] On October 29th he took seven children on a picnic to Hogg Island, dined on turkey and other fowls, and got home at sunset. More than a month later, the toll of conferences, visits, calls, sermons, being if not over, at least ended perforce, on November 22nd, he "set sail out of Boston Harbor an hour by Sun with a very fair wind." The next morning passengers were already in "great discomfort" from the northeast wind. "Beny Harris reads the 21 of the *Proverbs*, which is the first Chapter I heard read on Shipboard" was the first entry in his *Diary*.

His subsequent log of the six-week sea journey in stormy weather is a fair sample of winter sailing in one of the several hundred small ships that took the risk in those days with notable courage and seamanship. Seventeenth century sea-captains were a noble breed. The record of this voyage in the *America*, as the *Diary* tells it, is the tale of a small company of passengers who were acquaintances when they started, and who with captain and crew together would meet a succession of mishaps and near dangers by their joint labor, informed skill and patience. It is also the tale of daily Bible reading and psalm singing, no matter how strong the gale; of enthusiastic interest, as they watch rainbows, identify birds and sea creatures, catch two petrels to keep alive, and near the far shore hear news from ships they meet or sail with in consort.

In Samuel Sewall's account not a word of the monotony, no complaint of what must have been extreme cold, of the diet, in part supplied by themselves, of dark days with cabins shut and candles burning, windy days with cabins in confusion as trunks burst open with the back and forth motion of the ship. There were days in a violent northeaster, with no food possible, water in the cabins, clothing soaked; very "laborious days" by reason of hail, snow, wind and "a swoln sea all in a foaming breach," followed by nights without sleep. Winter discomfort, even danger, in seventeenth century calendars was merely a fact to be noted either on land or on sea; hardships were to be met; God was the author of both the storm and the rainbow that ended it. "May he fit us for what we are to meet with" was in letter and in spirit the prayer of passengers not on one ship alone. For Samuel Sewall, as for all other diary-keepers of his day, weather was an important item, seldom omitted, but usually entered without comment, as one of the facts in the day's life.

That he was homesick on this voyage is plain enough, and not only once. On the fifth day out he "Ait one of my wives Pastry, the remembrance of whom is ready to cut me to the heart. The Lord pardon and help me." [4] He records his dreams of her, once in a plain dress and white apron, handing him a piece of cake. Once he dreams of a child being born to her, and once of her death. Home was often in his thought, and it would be weeks yet before he could have his first word of news from New England. He spent many hours reading Dr. Manton and Dr. Preston, as comfort for separation from wife and family. Another book he had taken along was *Erasmus*, and he noted regretfully that water in the cabin had loosened the binding.

At midnight, one night after they had been out for a week, "the Ship being under a hard Gale of wind" the whipstaf was somehow "loosened from the Gooseneck," putting all in "great Consternation." "Turn out all hands" was the Captain's command, and turn out they all did. Several went below into the gunroom to steer, and "by God's blessing no great harm." Some of the men said, Sewall added, that "if she had not been a stiff ship she would have overset." The next day "a Sea shipped into the Cabin to our great startling and discomfort." Two days later there is more trouble with the whipstaf, and they "ly by" until repairs are made.[5] Once the main top mast is taken down to prepare for a tempestuous night. Similarly throughout the whole voyage, mishaps came, and always the passengers were as ready as the crew when a call came for sudden help. Acquiring skill in handling a boat was part of almost any New Englander's experience of growing up, and with skill came confidence in an emergency.

On December 4th, after another violent northeaster, "Kill a shoat." December 7th: "Breakfast on one of my wives Plum Cakes. Read Dr. Preston, Saints Support of sorrowful Siners. One of the Geese dyes yesterday, or today." On December 14th they began to see birds, also a number of strange fish; and on December 19th, a rainbow. In the evening of this day "Mr. Sampson set the Sun by the Compass." Passengers began to wager on the date they would first see England and they made a purse of thirty or forty shillings, New England money, for him who shall win. Samuel Sewall subscribed "an oblong Mexico piece of Eight." [6]

On December 25th they "see two Ships, one to windward, 'tother to Leeward," and a woodcock flies on board. Five days later they speak with a ship seven weeks from Barbadoes and are told, mistakenly, that the King is dead. In this region they begin to see many ships, exchange news with one from London, one from Ireland, and another from Barbadoes. Each ship has news, one of the landing of William of Orange. Captain Clark goes aboard one of these ships and returns with oranges and shaddock. These two ships sail in consort for a time.

Close by the Scylly Isles they nearly ran upon the rocks, "just upon our Larboard Bow, horrid, high, gaping Rocks." But they put on their light, "Trim'd sharp for our Lives," and escaped harm. On January 2nd they ate Simon Gates's goose, saw a gray linnet and a lark; on January 5th a flock of sparrows, and some said they saw a robin redbreast. On January 8th it was "the Lighthouse, that look't so slender, about the height of a man." On January 12th they met with a "Pink from Liverpool," and learned for a truth that the Prince of Orange had landed. The Isle of Wight and the "high white Cliffs" came into view. Samuel counted seven of them. On January 13th, the voyage was over. It was Sabbath. They landed at Dover, went ashore, and heard two sermons from Isaiah 66, 9.[7]

On the next morning a sightseeing tour began which lasted for months and would seem to have missed little that lay along the paths chosen. Sewall's record for the most part is a mere listing of the towns they passed through. He notes "some very good Buildings," a handsome courthouse and market place, a tavern where they drink or a river they cross. His small party arrived at Canterbury at night, but with time enough to "view the Cathedral." How much time, one wonders. As a boy of less than nine years, he had probably seen Winchester cathedral, near to his home, but if so, the memory would be dim after twenty-seven years. Were the majesty and

glory of Canterbury a memorable experience to him? If
so, he did not record it as such. In his fuller almanac
notes for this part of the journey, he added only that
"the Cathedral is a very lofty and magnificent building,
but of little use." [8] The remark is a window into a seventeenth century Boston view of much more than a skyline.
One learns much about New England culture of this far
day from this clipped *Diary* record.

In London he visited the Exchange first of all; thence
to the Temple, Whitehall, Westminster Abbey, Henry
VII chapel, St. James Park, all of which are merely
names in a list, but he stopped to record the text of Dr.
Sharpe's sermon before the Commons. He measured
the library of Gresham College and found it to be one
hundred and fifty feet long and eighteen feet wide. The
Guild Hall was fifty yards long and by his "yard-jointed
Rule," sixteen yards wide. St. Paul's was "a great and
excellent piece of work for the Arches and Pillars and
Porches." He also measured the Guild Hall stairs, stood
in the clock gallery and watched the pageantry attending
the choice of mayor. Sheriffs in their gold chains, alder-
men coming two by two, the mace carried before them,
the people shouting, "a Hall, a Hall" delighted his
eyes and ears. Here in London, as at home, such details
were seldom missed in his record. Streamers, flags, guns
on the Queen's birthday, bells for the birth of a son to
Princess Anne, made other high moments. The color
and ceremony of the entrance of the Dutch ambassadors
through streets "thwacked with people," fifty coaches
with six horses apiece, pages on foot, youths on horseback, was still another. His naïve remark that in spite of
the crowds watching the procession "yet little miss of
people in Fen Church and Lombard Streets" [9] tells as
much of Boston as of London. The London Artillery in

their buff clothes, feathers in their hats, and the silver headpieces of some in the White Regiment would be remembered for a long time.

With William Brattle he went to a concert in Covent Garden; a "Consort of Musick," he called it. There is evidence on various occasions during this trip and many times throughout his life that music satisfied, or at least spoke to Samuel Sewall, saying something that painting, architecture, and sculpture could not reach. His own word that he loved music to a fault is no exaggeration. The psalms sung in his home in childhood were probably partly responsible, laying a foundation for a lifetime of enjoyment and possibly more. At home his wife played on the virginals; he went to listen to Thomas Brattle's organ, and on Sunday he set the tune in the Old South. He probably had a clear, strong voice and a true pitch. His many words of pleasure in music make welcome interludes in his story. At Salisbury cathedral he asked the organist to play for him and his companions. In Hampshire he remarked that "Stoke people sing well." There are many such items.

Through the days and weeks that followed this first long excursion, Increase Mather and other New Englanders in London brought numerous invitations which opened English doors to him and enlarged his circle of acquaintance. There were many dinners, for which the food was unfailingly reported: a Neat's tongue, cheesecakes, raspberry wine, "a dish of Bacon with Pidgeons, Sauce, Beans and Cabbage," roast veal and strawberries, tarts, "Fowls and Bacon with Livers," "a Bullock's cheek," a "Dish of Salt Fish and a Piece of Mutton," currant suet pudding and "the fairest dish of Aples I have eat in England," "a Legg Mutton boiled and Colly-Flowers, Carrets, Rosted Fowls, and a dish of

Pease." [10] The list is long and each menu set down with a gourmet's pleasure.

Emanuel College at Cambridge had special emphasis in part for John Cotton and Thomas Hooker's sake, in part for the treasures displayed; among these a manuscript of Wyclif's translation of the Bible. He climbed to the roof, saw the town and Ely ten miles off. "In sum [he concluded] Cambridge is better than it shows for at first; the meanness of the Town-buildings, and most of the Colledges being Brick." At Oxford he found "Maudlin & Christ Ch. do most excell." Of the Bodleian Library he wrote, "The Galleries very magnificent about 44 of my Canes in length and near 8 in breadth. I lookt in one book which in Cuts sets forth the Glory of Old Rome." Corpus Christi Library was about the "bigness of our Chapel;" [11] that of Eton was sixty-nine feet long with four shelves. Always the library had a word, if only for its dimensions.

Invariably, wherever he went, he distributed sermons, at feastings, on calls, when bestowing gifts, as at home. He had come well supplied with Cotton Mather's sermons in particular and he gave them out while they lasted. He heard English sermons wherever he went, bought those in print for distribution at home. English church customs always had mention in the Sunday record. At. St. Helena's, the method of celebrating the Lord's Supper in its differences from New England caught his attention. He gave details, including the words Dr. Annesley said to him as he passed the cup, "Remember the death of Christ." The deacon refilled the cup and offered it to him.

At the Old Bailey he sat for three hours waiting for the jury to bring in four verdicts. "Rid to Tyburn, and saw eighteen Persons, 16 men and 2 Women fall." [12]

At Greenwich he looked through "glasses" and was shown the "Instruments of Observation." He swam in the Thames with Mr. Brattle, saw a dwarf and blessed God for his own stature, conferred with his agents, went to funerals, saw two culprits stand in the pillory, pelted with dirt, went into a Jewish graveyard at Mile End, drank a glass of beer with the keeper and hoped we would meet in heaven. He played ninepins; bought gifts. At the Chancellor's in Salisbury he lifted a four-month-old baby out of the cradle and kissed her.

The Samuel Sewall of these *Diary* pages is a somewhat different man from the New England councillor, the grave judge, the praecentor of the Old South, but in his appetite for new sermons, preached by new preachers, he is the man we know. Sermons have more space than cathedrals he had merely "time to view." Perhaps his enjoyment of majestic buildings expressed itself in his use of the yard measurement he carried, for it was always in his pocket, and the result in feet and inches was invariably entered in the day's record. Naturally enough town-houses, warehouses, market places, courthouses had chief emphasis. Art of all sorts, except music, is absent from the record. It had little to offer, for there was little to connect it with his twenty-seven years of New England living.

One of the best examples of his delight in music comes in his description of a tattoo played by the Watch at the burial of an ensign. He expressed it clearly in these words: "The tattoo with which the watch is set goes thus.

Durrera Dum

Durrera Dum

Durrera Dum

Dum dum   Dum Dum   Durrera Dum

Dum dum   Dum Dum   Durrera Dum
Durrera Dum

All three sets of drums take it one after another." [13]
One should like to know whether he attempted to explain and practice this tattoo with the drummers of the
Boston Artillery Company of which he was later the
captain. The answer is very probably yes.

On journey to Epping with Samuel Mather he read a
letter with news of the revolution against Andros in
Boston. His remark, "We were surpris'd with Joy," [14]
tells more of his resentment against the Andros regime
than he had dared to write even in his *Diary* entries in
Boston. He bought the broadside imprints sold by the
London hawkers, sent them to relatives in Hampshire
and to various English friends.

His visits in Hampshire were detailed in an almanac
record not copied into the *Diary*. His pleasure in these
family reunions and meetings with relatives known
previously only in letters was probably the pleasantest
part of the year's experience for him. Richard Dummer
was still alive. He names Uncle Richard and Cousin
Mary Stork as "the most kind of all my Relatives." The
many others he names make a large company. He rented
a horse "9 s/6 in full for his Hire," and journeyed from
town to town to visit many of them. There is obvious
excitement and pleasure also in his return to the remembered places of his childhood. He heard preaching
in churches at least familiar to him by name, lodged at
homes he knew as a schoolboy. Thence to Coventry,
home of the early Sewalls. He copied inscriptions of his
forbears from their tombs, heard his namesake, "Mr.
Shewell" preach, saw his "grt grandfather's name in

the City Hall without any alias," and "had 3 of the city Waits bid me good morrow with their wind Musick." [15]

From his own entries one gathers that he was of little help to Increase Mather in the charter cause. He speaks of being able to testify that Andros had raised money without an assembly, but though present at the appointed hour, he was given no opportunity to speak. He tried a second time, with no better fortune. At another time he went to Westminster to give evidence, but to no result. The inference is that Increase Mather may have been responsible for these slights, although he had put Sewall's name in as a witness. Sewall's word is "he seems plainly to be offended, and for my part I can't tell for what." He went to Hampton Court on May 9 and May 18, "to wait on the King and Council," when New England was being discussed, but he gives no details of these meetings. His remark on the charter proceedings that "our New England friends are in for Cakes and Ale, and we must doe all we may and swim or sink with them," [16] forecasts the outcome.

There is no detailed record of success in his effort to clear the title to his New England land possessions without paying the large sum exacted for the English patent. On April 29, shortly before his petition to return home, he wrote to Philip, Lord Wharton, but this letter was rather more a courtesy than a direct appeal and contains no specific reference to his own property interests. He merely pleads for a favorable vote in Parliament, "in doing which you will be a Partner with God, Who is wont to be concerned in relieving the Oppressed." [17] There may of course have been earlier and more specific letters.

The homeward journey was delayed because of the

war with France. As early as June 13, 1689, "We sign
a Petition for leave to go home." He had grown anxious,
and yet for greater safety, he waited. On August 13
and again on August 27 he went aboard the *America*,
and by September 14 had sailed only as far as Plymouth,
where he was obliged to wait until October 10th before
the convoy was permitted to accompany them. Rough
weather again, severe illness of a passenger, then of
several passngers, made the voyage anxious. At one
point, fearing he would be buried at sea, he added several provisions to his will, "If it should please God . . .
to put an End to my Life before I come to Boston." [18]

Things went better, however, toward the end of the
journey, and on November 15, one can feel the exulta-
tion in his word, "A good Cod was caught, And now we
have tasted afresh of American Fare." Ten days later
"At break of day . . . the Wind Carried away our
Main-top Mast." Eight feet of it were lost. Three days
later they were in the Latitude of Cape Anne. "A flock
of Isle a Shoales Ducks seen to day. Blessed be God who
has again brought me to a sight of New–England." [19]
Cape Anne was too difficult to weather, and the landing
was finally made on the Piscataqua River. Sewall rode
to Newbury where friends were "exceding glad to see
me, being surpris'd at my coming that way." This was on
November 29, 1689. He spent the Sabbath in Newbury
and returned to Boston, December 2nd.

Pleasure in his homecoming is accented on his pages
by mention of the gifts he had brought to his family, a
small cargo in themselves. They included three small
trunks with the letters and birth dates of his three oldest
children and one large trunk marked with nails H.S.,
presumably for Hannah, his wife. There were four
muffs, hats, biscuits, a barrel of books, liquors, cheese,

and much beside, suggesting his characteristic lavishness in family thoughtfulness and generosity.

On December 5th he took oath before General Bradstreet for his membership in the General Court, and was treated by the deputies. On January 3rd he treated them in return, and he was once again back in the official routine of a Boston executive's life. At home he read the morning chapter with the family and listened as the children read in their turn. His nine-year-old daughter Betty wept as she read Isaiah 24, and her father wept with her, probably at her weeping. He was back in the daily round of husband and father. On Sunday he set the tune in the Old South and recorded the sermon. No decisions of great moment appeared to be imminent. His life pattern was set as before, only perhaps more firmly.

His absence had covered one of the important years in New England history. On April 16, 1689, General Andros had written to Anthony Brockballs,

"There is a general buzzing among the people, great with expectation of their old charter, or they know not what." [20]

He left Boston and went to the fort. On April 18th Boston streets were filled with men and boys, armed with guns or clubs, all hurrying as to an appointed rendezvous. Suddenly drums beat and the officers of Andros not with him at the fort were arrested and put under guard. Dudley and "that blasted wretch Randolph" were lodged in the common jail.

Aged Governor Bradstreet and a number of former magistrates were escorted to the Council House and at noon from the balcony the "Declaration of the Gentlemen, Merchants and Inhabitants of Boston and the Counties adjacent" was read to the people gathered below. The fort was surrounded, Andros and those with him were disarmed, brought to the Town-House and put under guard. The next day they were removed to the Castle. The Andros dictatorship was over.

Former Governor Bradstreet and twenty-two others organized themselves into a "Council for the Safety and the Conservation of the Peace" with Bradstreet as President and Wait Winthrop as commander of the militia, while they waited to learn the "will of the people" as to their future course. Government under the old charter was their intention. On May 22nd at the convention convened by delegates of fifty-four towns, the former magistrates were put in charge of the government until word was received from England.

Meanwhile the order to proclaim William and Mary was received and performed in an outburst of public joy such as could hardly be matched in the memory of those who took part. The Crown, largely through Increase Mather, then in London, made investigation and on July 25th ordered Andros returned to England. Further settlement still lagged during the war with France, and attention to New England concerned chiefly the exposure of her northern frontiers to French assault. Samuel Sewall returned during stern fears over French and Indian outbreaks while the long parley over the charter continued in London. Had he not been away at the time of the revolt, he would undoubtedly have joined in it; but he would not have been one of those to inspire it. Now that it was accomplished, he justified the people's action in a pamphlet written jointly with Edward Rawson under the title, "The Revolution in New England Justified and the People there Vindicated," [21] from the aspersions cast upon them by Mr. John Palmer. It was printed in 1691. This was a strong, clear statement of New England's complete concur-

rence with the Church of England as to doctrine, and
disagreement as to liturgy and ceremonies only. It also
stated loyalty to King William and Queen Mary. The
body of the piece listed the matters objected against
Andros and others imprisoned with him, and the wrongs
done under the "ill government" of Andros, with the
oaths of those testifying to them. "Thus did *Sir Edmund
Androsse* and his creatures . . . commit a rape on a
whole colony."

In April of 1690 he spent two weeks on a journey
with William Stoughton to New York as one of the
commissioners to attend a meeting with delegates from
all the colonies looking toward plans for their mutual
safety. In his own words it was a journey "in great heaviness of my spirit," [22] whether because of the discomfort
of travel or the responsibility he bore as a Massachusetts
delegate, he does not say, but possibly both reasons contributed. He made few journeys in America so long as
this. Except for the frequent visits to Newbury, usually
by boat, and later the long horseback travel as he rode
the judicial circuit, he was a neighborhood traveller.
The English journey was the only excursion of its kind
in his life. There is exhilaration, even excitement in
many of the *Diary* pages that tell its story. Release from
the familiar Boston routine, crowding new scenes, and
complete freedom from the responsibility of public office
had given him a year of almost youthful pleasure, such
as he had not had in his twenties. Now he had come
back to grim times with an early middle age immediately
ahead of him.

EIGHT

On the Bench in Salem Village

THE HYSTERIA of the witchcraft chapter was almost at hand, although to understand the "woeful chain of consequences" it would always be in our history, one must read the signs long backward. By the time Samuel Sewall returned from the English journey, it was already too late to check its course, and before he was appointed one of the judges to conduct the trials, time had quite run out. Salem jails were crowded with those condemned by their neighbors, hearings were already being held before local magistrates, and all New England was aroused. At this point legal action by the colony of Massachusetts, not the town of Salem, seemed the way out. By that path would come tragedy.

On May 14, 1692, Sir William Phips arrived with the new charter Massachusetts had waited for since 1684. He was immediately told what was happening in Salem, and on the advice of his Councillors, and as one of his first acts, he appointed seven Councillors of a Special Court of Oyer and Terminer to try those accused. William Stoughton was made Chief Justice and his associates, of whom any five were to constitute the Bench, were Jonathan Corwin, Bartholomew Gedney,

John Hathorne, John Richards, Nathaniel Saltonstall, Peter Sergeant, Samuel Sewall, and Wait Still Winthrop. Nathaniel Saltonstall refused to serve, and Jonathan Corwin was put in his place. The first sitting having been arranged for June 2, Sir William Phips departed to the Indian wars in the north.

According to the provisions of the new charter, the General Court was to approve the Governor's appointments to any special courts such as this one. General Court was not in session until June 8th of this year, but in the urgency of the Salem situation, the judges held their first session prior to this date. Authority for so doing was the original Body of Liberties of the colony which had been the basis for court action during the period between one charter and the other. The first victim was executed on June 10th, two days before the General Court approved the judges appointed and voted in the phrasing of the original charter "to continue all laws not repugnant to England." The charge of illegality for the action of the first court session scarcely holds, since the Body of Liberties had been the authority invoked during the years of waiting for the issuing of the provincial charter.

Along with his fellow judges, Samuel Sewall brought to the trial sessions an almost unchallenged heritage of belief in the reality of witches as the devil's agents. To seventeenth century men and women of enlightenment, as well as to the ignorant, witches were willing agents of Satan, pledged to overthrow God's kingdom on earth. Their presence in any community was a *sign* the elect ignored at their peril. Every New England child had grown up knowing that Satan's dearest hope was to conquer New England for himself. This theme had been persistent in every pulpit since the first landing. In the

Mother Land and in Europe the reality of witches was a belief centuries old. First arguments against so long-established a belief are impotent. Believers have no ears to hear them. To have denied the reality of these evil agents in 1692 would have meant to question also a literal heaven and hell, all angels, all devils, fire, brimstone, golden streets and even the Judgment Day itself. Witches were part of the total fabric of accepted truth, except to the very few as yet silent doubters, who were aware that across the sea this idea was just beginning to be challenged in print.

Massachusetts colony from the beginning had followed the specific statutes against witches from the reigns of Henry VI, Henry VIII, Elizabeth and James I, and had made witchcraft a capital offence. Mosaic law was the warrant. In stumbling human literalness they had obeyed Exodus 22, 18, "Thou shalt not suffer a witch to live," as God's own fiat. In the Massachusetts Body of Liberties this statute follows immediately after the provision for punishment of idolatry, which is article I. No II reads,

"If any man or woman be a witch (that is hath or consulteth with a familiar spirit) they shall be put to death." [1]

This legal definition of a witch was adhered to throughout the Salem trials.

Only rough estimates are possible, but the suggested figure of some 300,000 executions and burnings in Europe and the British Isles during the century of the Salem Village outbreak is perhaps an understatement. Against this towering figure, the nineteen deaths on the scaffold and one under heavy stones in New England, 1692, might seem a small total in proportion to the shame these deaths have spread over our colonial story, but as to the heaviness of that shame, let any history of New England testify. Our first century wrote no darker page.

There had been sporadic witchcraft cases in New England prior to 1692, but surprisingly few in comparison with the disasters that might so naturally have been attributed to evil spirits in human flesh. John Winthrop recorded the "malignant touch" of Margaret Jones, a practicing physcian in Charlestown, executed in 1648.[2] Her death was grimly remembered in Connecticut because of a "great tempest" that came at the hour she was on the gallows. Ann Hibbins, widow of a Representative to the General Court in Boston, and agent of the colony, had fallen victim to the malicious gossip of her neighbors and had been executed.[3] Her husband's services to Massachusetts colony, her own wit (was it in too great excess of wit belonging to those who maligned her?) and perhaps also her large estate had made her indictment and death for witchcraft the subject of some controversy and some denunciation, but 1655 was still too early for skepticism wide enough or healthy enough to call either the charge or the death penalty into question. There had been various other single cases, enough to keep witchcraft always in the foreground of one's fears and to account for the frequent mention of it in Sunday sermons. No one of these cases, however, had aroused widespread hysteria. In England a condemned witch had been burned as late as 1682, only ten years before the Salem panic. This seems to be the last witchcraft death on record in the British Isles.

Probable causes of the Salem hysteria are easy to assemble. Among them, Cotton Mather's printed account of the supposed "afflictions" of the four children of John Goodwin of Boston in 1688 is perhaps one of the most

direct. In a time of depression and deep anxiety over loss
of the charter and uncertainty as to New England's
future government, this supposed tale of Satan in our
midst gave concreteness to the feeling that something
was very wrong with New England. To read such a book
at such a time meant also to watch for similar manifestations in other families. The four "afflicted children"
(two boys and two girls, the eldest thirteen), as reported
by Cotton Mather, barked, purred, mewed, moved as
though with wings, and took on many other strange behaviors. One girl rode herself up the stairs as though on
horseback, simulated being in the oven — perspiration
dropping from her face — or choking with an invisible
noose around her neck. Most convincing of all her tricks,
to the orthodox, was that she was struck senseless at the
sight of the *Assembly's Catechism,* John Cotton's *Milk
for Babes,* and other orthodox books, but could read the
Book of Common Prayer, popish or Quaker books without a qualm. Surely Satan was within her. Parents,
neighbors, physicians, ministers were in consternation
and baffled to find any other cause than "bewitched" for
such doings. Who was the witch? Goody Glover, the girl
answered, and Goody Glover died on the gallows.

Cotton Mather's account was widely and immediately
read. It was entitled, *Late Memorable Providences Relating to Witchcrafts and Possessions,*[4] for its day a title
to invite readers. Richard Baxter, who wrote the recom-
mendatory preface, testified that he had seen no reason
to question these strange behaviors as proofs of demoniac power. Neither did many of the New England
clergy who, fortified by Baxter's eminence, passed the
book on to others. Its success lay in the circumstantial
detail. Cotton Mather had taken the oldest girl, clever-
est of the four children, into his home for a time, while

he wrote his account of her antics, and for novelty alone, they are arresting. Read as "bewitchment" by her credulous contemporaries, they make a story of strange powers at work. Read today, against a heritage of disbelief in witches, they reveal on every page the adroit cleverness of this child, her flattery of Cotton Mather, and his (to us) amazing blindness not to detect her trickery, while his pen was in his hand.

That other children, hearing about the Goodwins, might imitate their behaviors, apparently occurred to no one. However, that is precisely what happened in Salem Village, quickly becoming the first chapter in the sad "delusion." Irresponsible children had also been the "evidence" in the much publicized Bury St. Edmunds case in England, tried before Sir Matthew Hale twenty-eight years earlier.[5] Among the "marvels" those children had seen were invisible mice, which when caught and thrown into the fire had exploded with loud noises and flashes of fire. Amy Drury and Rose Callender were named as witches and tried on evidence such as this. Sir Matthew, eminent man of law, merciful beyond most, had been deeply affected by the testimony against them, and in his charge to the jury did not sum up the evidence, but left the room with a prayer that God "would direct their Heads." *Guilty* was the verdict and the two women had died. The eminence of Sir Matthew had made both his action and the jury's verdict in the case authoritative to other judges and juries. The Salem Village judges were well familiar with it.

"Afflicted children" had been the exciting cause of other witchcraft hysteria as well. In popular interpretation the assumed innocence of the very young made their supposed "affliction" a pitiable proof of the devil's dark designs, and the adult pursuit of their tormentors was

swift and without mercy more often than not. As to the
Salem children themselves, no doubt in the beginning
they may have enjoyed the excitement of being central
figures before an audience, and after they were all but
forced to name their supposed tormentors, it was too late
to stop what their antics had started. Perhaps sometimes
they were frightened into keeping on, perhaps in the
tumult which ensued, they half-believed their own supposed bewitchment. One had best leave three-century-
old motives alone and keep to the facts. In the Salem
story we also have the adult confession of Anne Putnam,
the twelve-year-old leader of the "afflicted children."

Her two younger accomplices were Elizabeth Parris,
nine-year-old daughter of Samuel Parris, the village
minister, and Abigail Williams, his niece, who lived in
the household. The parsonage was the place where it all
started. Two older girls, Nancy Walcot, daughter of
Deacon Walcot, and Mercy Lewis, employed in the
household of the Rev. George Burroughs, one of those
executed, were also members of the group. Four other
young women, Elizabeth Booth, Susannah Sheldon,
Nancy Warren and Sarah Churchill, were also part of
the story. As it can be pieced together from many fragments of testimony, the children and young girls had apparently met together occasionally in the winter of
1691/92 in the parsonage parlor to read books about
palmistry, magic and spiritism. The Parris bookshelves
would very likely have held books on occult phe-
nomena, and besides, such books were in circulation in
any New England parish. William Perkins's *Discourse
of the Damned Act of Witchcraft*, 1608, perhaps Joseph
Glanvil's *Saducismus Triumphatus*, or *Full and Plain
Evidence concerning Witches and Apparitions*, Richard
Burton's *The Certainty of the World of Spirits*, were

there also, as Cotton Mather had imported them. His *Memorable Providences*, telling of the Goodwin children, would hardly need the support of print; it was a conversation piece. If Samuel Parris knew of these meetings, he did not admit the knowledge, not even after the excitement put the parsonage in the center of everyone's thought.

Details of what went on at these meetings are too vague and scant for certain statement. They had probably begun in a natural curiosity about strange behaviors, fostered very likely by the contributions of Tituba, a West Indian servant in the house, and John Indian, her husband, both of whom would have been able to add bizarre details from their distant native land. It appeared at the trials that at the direction of Mary Sibley, Tituba had made a loathsome cake, supposedly possessing magic power. After the trials began, Mary Sibley was reprimanded in church meeting, and Tituba and John Indian were deported, but only after their testimony had done irreparable harm. The skill of the children in their muscular controls, bodily contortions, rigidity under pinpricking, pinching and other tests, their tongue-swallowing, apparent dislocation of joints, shrieking and moaning in strange keys need afford no mystery. Diligent practice and the desire to amaze others explain them easily enough, and suspicion of a devil's agent in such behaviors blinded the observer to any natural explanation. The best item of performance would seem to have been their ability to execute their tricks in perfect unison.

To later view, it would seem that Samuel Parris, father, uncle, and neighbor of the three principals, could hardly have failed to know what was going on in his own house and could have stopped it all, but he did not. Instead, he invited neighboring ministers to witness these strange "afflictions" of the children. Private fasts were held at the parsonage and guests spent hours in wondering parley and much prayer. Physicians were called in and admitted being baffled. The ministers departed, carrying the news to their own parishes and spreading the suspicion. Samuel Parris, who has been seriously accused for his part in the whole affair, was very probably only deluded.

He was not a minister by the usual training, but had been a merchant in the West Indies before deciding to preach and accepting the call to Salem Village. In terms of village peace, he had made sad mistakes before the 1692 crisis in his parish. He had been excessively concerned over a guaranteed salary increase for the future, had demanded title to the parsonage land as his own possession, and when refused, had instituted a lawsuit. He had also gone to law over his wood supply. The parish had been riven by party factions before his coming, and the intra-mural disputes over each of his demands had widened the breach between the parties. Perhaps a man of tact and Christian zeal could not have healed them; certainly one using such business methods to drive a hard bargain could not.[6] The congregation had grown deeply restive even before the suspicion of the devil's presence among them had precipitated a panic. All classes of members were involved in the previous unrest: half-way members, covenant members and even the unchurched of the village had taken sides, a condition which invited to crisis during the trials.

Excitement over the parsonage children had reached a pitch before March 24th, when Deodat Lawson, former pastor in the village, was announced as the preacher. Everyone came, including many from the country around. No one present would ever forget that sermon. The Rev. Mr. Lawson had been back in Salem Village for five days, had seen the apparent "sufferings" of the "afflicted children" demonstrated individually and in a group. They were present in the meetinghouse that morning and interrupted him by their strange outcries. His text was Zechariah 3, 2: "And the Lord said unto Satan, The Lord rebuke thee, O Satan; even the Lord that hath chosen Jerusalem rebuke thee: is not this a brand plucked out of the fire?" Truly the text was Zechariah, but the application was to Salem Village.

"You are therefore to be deeply humiliated, and sit in the dust, considering the signal hand of God is singling out this place, this poor village, for the first seat of Satan's tyranny, and to make it (as 'twere) the rendezvous of devils, where they muster their infernal force."

He addressed the local dignitaries who were present in their panoply of office.

"Let us admit no parley, give no quarter: let none of Satan's forces or furies be more vigilant to hurt us than we are to resist and repress them, in the name, and by the spirit, grace, and strength of our Lord Jesus Christ."
"Do all that in you lies to check and rebuke Satan; endeavoring, by all ways and means that are according to the rule of God, to discover his instruments in these horrid operations." [7]

The effect of these impassioned counsels, not from a stranger, but from one who had been pastor among them, was to add recklessness to action that had already gone past rational judgment. As to Deodat Lawson himself, one can only judge his unwisdom as that of a man in whom for the moment knowledge of human nature was forgotten, as he gave rein to his own irresponsible zeal. Those who heard were thus further prepared to act irresponsibly also.

Before Samuel Sewall and his fellow judges made their first journey empowered to conduct the trials, more than a hundred suspected persons were in jail, the town was obsessed by fear and torn apart with suspicion. Husbands wondered about wives, wives about husbands. Everyone watched everyone else, especially their own children, in search of evidence for bewitchment. On March 1st, Tituba confessed herself to be a witch. Two weeks later Martha Corey and Rebecca Nourse were named by the "afflicted children" and sent to prison. On April 3rd, Samuel Parris preached on the text, "Have I not chosen you twelve and one of you is a devil?" Sarah Cloyse, sister of Rebecca Nourse, left the meetinghouse. As she went out the door, it was slammed behind her, presumably by the wind. This was evidence. She too was taken to prison. All three of these women were eminent for their piety and godliness.

Not to ignore the local reasons for this state of affairs which are plain enough to see, or to quarrel with them, it is also well to place Salem Village at this hour of near tragedy within the provinciality of New England in 1692. Boston, its largest city, possibly had five thousand inhabitants. For all except the very few, especially in the towns and villages a day's journey by boat or horseback from Boston, local concerns, explained by local interpreters, had little chance to be placed in a wider perspective. At the right moment, some authoritative voice perhaps from Boston, from the throne of King William, or a voice from the Royal Society, searching for realistic answers to marvels of many sorts, could have brought an atmosphere in which the inquiry into the antics of the supposedly "afflicted children" might have been *What* instead of *Who*, but no such avenue was open to Salem Village in 1692, and no voice spoke. What was happening to the parsonage children filled the earth and sky of village thought. *Who* is hurting you was the first and the persistent question in trial after trial. The circumference of the parish became almost the boundary of the world. No wonder that local happenings gained gigantic size and importance within so limited a circumference. In part they can be understood when this tight boundary is taken into account.

It is well also to read the whole story against the current sermon background, familiar to any child in the village, as well as to their parents. So long as no name was named in the long list of *signs* that the devil is loose amongst us, witchcraft lay quietly among the other signs. But let a local name be named and the teaching of a lifetime sprang into quick life. An unfamiliar sign in the preacher's list would have awakened no panic. It is what is already long familiar that becomes powerful when something immediate gives it fresh application. Proofs that God's smile had faded and that He was already punishing New England were numerous enough for every family in the village to have been touched by one woe or another. Locusts that ate the crops, smallpox that came again and again and was present that winter, wrecked vessels, burned houses and barns, drowned children, all were current. Most of all, the precious charter was gone and a new governor was in the chair. Spurred by Deodat Lawson's phrases, "the first seat of Satan's tyranny," the "rendezvous of devils," Salem Village became a concrete plan of action, not for herself alone, but to rid New England of their presence.

At the time of his appointment to the Court of Oyer and Terminer, Samuel Sewall was forty years old. Too much has been made of the assumption that he and his fellow judges were without legal training as a qualification for judging. Truly enough they had no formal training. Sewall had been a member of the General Court for seven years, and as a magistrate, he would have had considerable experience in dealing with those accused of misdemeanors. Under the colonial charter, the General Court exercised jurisdiction in all criminal cases for which a special court was not appointed. Later he imported books on English law and became one of the best equipped of Massachusetts judges in his day, but in 1692 this was still in the future. There was a strong vein of superstition in his nature, and he could accept as fact illogical details of supposed demoniac possession such as tradition had made familiar. So could his fellow judges.

To search his *Diary* for details of record for what he saw and heard during this fevered time is to be disappointed. His entries concerning Salem Village are few and brief. On April 11, 1692, more than a month before the arrival of Sir William Phips and his appointment as judge, he went to Salem with Thomas Danforth, Deputy Governor, and five members of his Council: James Russell, John Hathorne, Isaac Addington, Samuel Appleton and Jonathan Corwin. They went unofficially. The occasion was a hearing in the crowded meeting-house, before local Salem authorities, at which Sarah Cloyse and Elizabeth Procter were being examined by Samuel Parris. The "afflicted children" were present. John Indian, Mary Walcott, Abigail Williams and Anne Putnam were asked questions, framed by Samuel Parris and recorded by him. Almost unfailingly, the question asked implied the answer.
(Of Anne Putnam)

"Anne Putnam, doth this woman hurt you?"
"Yes, Sir: a great many times."

Then the accused looked upon them, and they fell into fits.

"She does not bring the book to you, does she?"
"Yes, sir; often, and saith she hath made her maid set her hand to it."

(Of Abigail Williams)

"Abigail Williams, does this woman hurt you?"
"Yes, sir, often."
"Does she bring the book to you?"
"Yes."
"What would she have you do with it?"
"To write in it, and I shall be well."

(Of John Indian)

"John, who hurt you?"
"Goody Procter first, and then Goody Cloyse."
"What did she do to you?"
"She choked me, and brought the book."
"How oft did she come to torment you?"
"A good many times, she and Goody Cloyse."
"Where did she take hold of you?"
"Upon my throat, to stop my breath."
"What did Goody Cloyse do to you?"
"She pinched and bit me till the blood came." [8]

Asked similar questions, Mary Walcott fell into her fits at intervals. At each time of the fit she was carried near enough to the supposed witch to be able to touch her body at some point. Immediately the fit subsided, as according to belief, the diabolical fluid flowed back into the witch's body. The examination went on until the fit came again.

At the trial before Sir Matthew Hale in 1664 the "afflicted" ones were blindfolded at this point in the proceedings, and touched not the supposed witch, but the clerk of the court. Their suffering ceased immediately and their falseness was revealed. Had this test been applied in Salem Village, it might have brought the beginnings of skepticism to some on the bench, but apparently it occurred to no one to apply tests of any sort to the witnesses or even to cross examine them.

When Samuel Parris had asked his quota of questions of each "afflicted" person, he turned to the accused women.

"What do you say, Goody Procter, to these things?"

Her reply is the only one of the afternoon, not implied in the question asked.

"I take God in heaven to be my witness, that I know nothing of it, no more than the child unborn." Similarly, the eloquence of Martha Carrier, at a later session, in her five words, "I have not done it." To the accusation that she had looked on the black man, "I know none." [9]

Samuel Sewall quotes none of this and supplies no details. His entry on the April 11th experience is a single sentence.

"Went to Salem, where, in the Meeting-house, the persons accused of Witchcraft were examined; was a very great Assembly; 'twas awfull to see how the afflicted persons were agitated." [10] On July 30, 1692, he mentions the escape of Mrs. Cary from Salem jail, and on August 19th, the execution of five victims on Gallows Hill: Martha Carrier, George Burroughs, John Williard, John Procter, and George Jacob.

"Mr. Mather says they all died by a Righteous Sentence. Mr. Burrough by his Speech, Prayer, protestation of his Innocence, did much move unthinking persons, which occasions their speaking hardly concerning his being executed." [11]

The Rev. George Burroughs had been a Harvard student with Sewall, had been a dinner guest at his home several years before his execution, on November 18, 1685 and on January 21, 1691, had preached at private meetings which Samuel Sewall attended. In the margin of this execution entry in the *Diary* are the words "Dolefull Witchcraft." These are the only references in his record to the witchcraft proceedings while they were taking place.

On July 20, 1692, in a letter to Cousin Hull in London, he wrote, "Am perplexed p[er] witchcrafts: six persons have already been condemned and executed in Salem." [12] He makes no mention of attending any of the executions and presumably did not, as he had done on other occasions. His silence in the *Diary* is not significant, as he makes many omissions of what might naturally seem to cry for a personal record. The phrase "Dolefull Witchcraft" might suggest a question in his own mind, but may of course have been added to the entry later.

The dogmatic insistence of Chief Justice Stoughton that the devil could not take the appearance of the spectre of an innocent person seems to have been openly contradicted by the other judges, as also by Increase and Cotton Mather and the larger body of ministers. Many words were spent on this controversial point, and had the majority prevailed against Stoughton, there would have been no limp bodies hanging from the scaffolds on Gallows Hill. It was the testimony of the "afflicted" that the spectres of the accused had appeared when they were far away, going about their daily tasks or asleep in their beds, that condemned them at the trials. The details are fantastic: spectres in the head of a blue boar, a cat, in the air, unbodied, recalled as seen even years before the trials which were going on. Read for this "spectre detail" through a dozen testimonies, conviction on these grounds passes all rational acceptance, except for a time when rational judgment on the bench as well as in the crowded assembly was laid to sleep.

One would think also that the duplication, time after time, of this flimsy spectral testimony in its limited range, of the little black man, the Red book, the little yellow bird sitting on the beam of the meetinghouse or on the rim of the minister's hat, wherever condemnation could be helped by it, would have lost its effectiveness and power to awe even those whose reason was elsewhere. Even more, the precisely identical writhings, stiffenings, strange moanings and screamings, dislocation of joints of the "afflicted children" on the floor. But no. The condemned were prosecuted by the very judges who should have tested the evidence, but apparently the veracity of the children was never even questioned. A little of the seadog language of John Alden, son of John and Priscilla, might have opened some eyes, but when accused, he had the wit to escape from jail, and to be telling his friends, not the court, what he thought of being confronted by a "lot of wenches" he had never seen before, who were calling him a witch.

The drama of accusation, condemnation, execution lasted for four months. Court sessions were held in June, August and September. There were nineteen executions on Gallows Hill and one death in the open field under

heavy stones, heaped on Giles Corey's chest. He had refused to speak, and for being "mute," met this almost
unbelievably cruel fate. It had all been a brief chapter,
measured in time, and small in total numbers, if put
beside the scores of dying from other human causes in
the length of a single day; but in New England history
it was a story of tragedy lifetimes long, not only for the
survivors of those who died, but for all the village and
for all of New England so long as her history is written.
A tale of human folly in a time of terror.

After the fever had cooled, it became apparent that
there had been those in Salem, as well as all over the
colony, who had believed in the innocence of the condemned. Testimonials had been submitted during the
trials, but the judges would not consider them. There
were also those who suspected the "afflicted children"
of fraud and trickery, but speech in this direction was
less open and confident. Cotton Mather's account of the
Goodwin children was everyone's knowledge, and the
Salem children were of the pastor's household. Samuel
Parris was up there beside the bench taking down the
testimony. In the trial sessions there appears to have
been little doubt that the children were suffering, as they
performed their tortures, while the WHO hurts you
and WHY do you hurt these children were being asked
over and over of the suspected. The presence of the five
judges sitting high before the packed meetinghouse, red-
robed, solemn, and their own pastor as interrogator, was
such a scene as had never been witnessed in Salem Village before, and was impressive in proportion. These
judges in their panoply of office were the highest judicial authority in the colony. The drama of the scene
itself offers plenteous explanation for the violence of the
furor it created.

The whole episode, in the fact, in its blindness and
hysteria, might have broken out in any equally self-con-
tained and fairly remote New England village. In every
detail except the speed with which it ended, it was
typical and not unique. The court sat for the last time
on September 17th, and on September 22nd, eight persons who had attested their innocence were executed on
Gallows Hill. Eight more had been tried on September
9th and 17th, but by confessing that they were witches
they saved their lives. Either to be an accuser or to confess were the two ways of safety. Confession, of course,
had basic theological warrant, and was resorted to often.
But not by such as Mary Easty. "I cannot, I dare not,
belie my own soul," she said, and died for it.[13]

The Salem jail was full of those still awaiting trial,
but by the January session that would hear them, many
things had changed. The "afflicted persons" had over-
reached themselves and named men and women in high
places: the wife of Governor Phips, who had secured a
pardon for one condemned; the Rev. Samuel Willard,
one of the most outspoken against the trials and against
spectral evidence, which he called "the devil's own testimony." The absurdity of such evidence, by which no one
was safe anywhere, was beginning to be seen in a quite
different light. Men and women, who had not dared
to lift their voices in favor of the condemned, offered
testimonials over their own signatures. Residents of
Salem Village began to think what they had done. Godly
Rebecca Nourse, aged, with a life of piety and kind
deeds behind her; what had she done amiss? She had
stayed away from meeting after one of the children had
interrupted the pastor during prayer. Goody Cloyse,
what had she done? Left the meetinghouse during the
sermon on "One of you is a devil." At the trial she had

fainted from either exhaustion or strain, when John Indian had said she had bitten him until the blood ran, drank it, and passed it on to others. "There is a yellow bird flying around her head," one of the children had screamed. Condemnation had followed and she had been executed. Ministers began to speak out more openly against such evidence as basis for a verdict of guilt.

When the court convened on January 3, 1692/93, it was difficult to get convictions without spectre testimony, but Chief Justice Stoughton had signed the warrant for the execution of eight more of the fifty prisoners under trial. Their graves were dug, when a messenger from Governor Phips arrived with reprieve for the eight and for three more. He also discharged all who were in jail, a number as large as the space of the jail could hold. Chief Justice Stoughton was indignant, and left the court, saying,

"We were in a way to have cleared the land of them; who is it that obstructs the cause of Justice, I know not; the Lord be merciful to the country." [14]

The "afflicted" children and young women suffered no more. They were not punished for their fraud, but Salem Village was not hospitable to them thereafter. Some of them sought oblivion elsewhere. Some changed their names in marriage. Years later Anne Putnam, leader of the children, now aged twenty-six, confessed and became a church member. As a confession, her statement is miscalled, since she did not really take the blame for what she had done, but said she was "deluded by Satan." This was on August 25, 1706, in a meetinghouse packed to the doors. The Rev. Joseph Green, successor to Samuel Parris, read her statement, while she stood in her place and when he had finished, acknowledged it to be hers. Her denial of any belief in communications from the devil at the time of her deceit had its importance for her day, although to have been "deluded by the devil," as she stated, left him, in current belief, still free to delude others.[15]

One might expect that Samuel Sewall would have left some record in his *Diary* of his own change of view, but he disappoints us. The day before the Court adjourned, he noted the confession of Dorcas Hoar. "This is the first condemned person who has confess'd." The next day he spoke of five men who met at his house to discuss publishing "Some Trials of the Witches." On October 15th, he reported a discussion with "Mr. Danforth" at Cambridge, in which he said there could be no further procedure in the Court except there be "some better consent of Ministers and People." [16] The public mood was changing. On October 26th a bill was sent in calling for a "Fast and Convocation of Ministers to determine the right way as to the Witchcrafts." It failed to pass; there were twenty-nine Noes and thirty-three Yeas. Sewall's comment that the Court of Oyer and Terminer count themselves thereby dismissed was correct. On October 29th, Governor Phips said, "It must fall."

On November 22nd there is a hint of unease in his entry, as he prays that God would pardon his "Sinfull Wanderings . . . choose and assist our Judges, and vindicate the late Judges, consisting with his Justice and Holiness &c., with Fasting." [17] It is apparent in this entry that he knows he is in line for a Judgeship. On December 6th he was chosen a Justice of the Superior Court.

Four years later, when proposal for a fast was again being talked of, he recalled that when the proposal had been made in 1692, "I doe not know that ever I saw the Council run upon with such a height of Rage before." [18] A second proposal had been made and also had failed to carry in the Council. A third attempt was made on December 11, 1696, and was concurred on December 17th. The date for the fast was set for Thursday, January 14th. A majority voted Yea. "I consent," said William Stoughton, hitherto an opposer.

This fast was held admittedly to ask God's forgiveness for what had been done about witches. This was four years after the last prisoners had been tried or freed. The proclamation mentioned specific calamities from which the province was suffering, and assumed there were specific sins for which God is angry and for which he expects forgiveness to be sought. Four years of course is a long time for any single event to hold the interest of the public, and the witchcraft trials did not, although there were few who had been old enough to share the intensity of excitement in 1692 who ever forgot that six-month panic. There was no need to remind them of the facts. After four years everything had been said and felt. Emotions had cooled long since, but everyone remembered.

From a few hints in his *Diary* and letters it is apparent that Samuel Sewall had been troubled. When on September 16th, the Governor, his Council and the Assembly had held a day of prayer in the Town-House, he wrote that Samuel Willard "spake smartly at last about the Salem Witchcrafts, and that an order had been suffer'd to come forth by Authority to ask God's pardon." There had been two deaths in Sewall's household during 1696, an abortive son on May 22nd, and little Sarah on December 23rd. She was buried on the 25th. Six of his children lay dead in the tomb. Wherein had he sinned? Was God angry with him? His thought of sin and disaster was always an equation. God kept unceasing watch over His children, punishing and rewarding them according to their deserts. Two more deaths; what did it mean? The simplicity of his reasoning seems childish indeed, but it was not his alone. It was a heritage as well as a current sermon view. He was finding the application of the text to his own life.

On December 24th, the day after little Sarah had died, Sam, his eldest son, was reading to his father in Latin, Matthew 12, 6–12. "The seventh verse did awfully bring to mind the Salem Tragedie," [19] Sewall wrote down for the day. It was his only entry. The verse reads, "But if ye had known what this meaneth, I will have mercy, and not sacrifice, ye would not have condemned the guiltless." On the next day he wrote, "We bury our little daughter." He spent some time in the tomb, where Father and Mother Hull, Cousin Quincy, and his six children lay. He had given order that little Sarah's coffin be set at her grandmother's feet.

When the fast of Thursday, January 16th, was held, he was in his pew, and as Samuel Willard walked slowly up the aisle to the pulpit Samuel Sewall put in his hand the Bill of Contrition for his own error in the witchcraft trials. He included a copy in his *Diary*, with the heading,

"Copy of the Bill I put up on the Fast Day, giving it to Mr. Willard as he Pass'd by, and standing up as he read it, and bowing when finished; in the Afternoon."

It was a noble gesture, completely in line with the custom of the day, established for two generations. To express private joy in the birth of a child, sorrow for a death in the family, anxiety for a journey to come or thanks for one safely accomplished, this way was always open. Bills had been read almost every Sunday in nearly every meetinghouse in New England since the first one had been built. Samuel Sewall's acknowledgment of error on this occasion was a high point in personal courage, dignity and humility. The meetinghouse in which he had worshipped since his young manhood was the place in which

"To take the Blame and shame of it, asking pardon of men, and especially desiring prayers that God who has unlimited Authority, would pardon that sin and all his other sins; personal and Relative."

He did not oversay his contrition or understate the sin he acknowledged. The straight line of his simple statement must have been moving to the congregation of this Thursday fast. He was one of the leading men of Boston and known to all. One hopes that the burden in his mind and conscience for four years was eased as he sat down. At least in this statement of error he wrote the final word in the witchcraft chapter by those who had part in it. That none of the other judges took this chance makes his word no less history's than his own.

An act of penance can do nothing to right the wrong committed, but it can dignify a human life and possibly lift the man who performs it to higher ground and help him to expect more of himself. One thinks perhaps inevitably, of aging Samuel Johnson, standing with bared head for an hour on the site of the bookstall kept by his father in Uttoxeter many years before. As a sixteen-year-old boy Samuel Johnson had refused to keep the stall for a day when his father was ill, and now as an old man he had come back to the same spot, in inclement weather, and amid the jeers of bystanders "to do away with the sin of this disobedience." This was nearly a century after Samuel Sewall had been laid to sleep in the Old Granary Burying Ground. His Bill of error belongs in his life story, in his own words. Here it is.

"Samuel Sewall, sensible of the reiterated strokes of God upon himself and family; and being sensible, that as to the Guilt contracted upon the opening of the late Commission of Oyer and Terminer at Salem (to which the order for this day relates) he is, upon many accounts, more concerned than any that he knows of, Desires to take the Blame and shame of it, asking pardon of men, And especially desiring prayers that God, who has an Unlimited Authority, would pardon that sin and all other his sins, personal and Relative; And according to his infinite Benignity, and Sovereignty, not Visit the sin of him, or of any other, upon himself or any of his, nor upon the land: But that He would powerfully defend him against all Temptations to Sin, for the future: and vouchsafe him the efficacious, saving Conduct of his Word and Spirit." [20]

To review this unhappy Salem episode in the life of a good man three centuries later calls for neither condemnation nor excuse. Both have been offered Samuel Sewall many times according to the perspective of historians who have told the story over once again. It is a story calling only for the interpretation of historical fact in the light of its own time and place, not of lifetimes later. Most men belong to their own times, and in their thinking they deserve to be understood through the overhanging ideas of that time and place, and the actions these ideas bring to pass. In no chapter of his seventy-eight years was Samuel Sewall more a seventeenth century Bostonian than in his share in the Salem Witchcraft Trials.

NINE

On the Bench in the Superior Court

IMMEDIATELY after the dissolution of the Special Court of Oyer and Terminer, Samuel Sewall was named one of the judges of the Superior Court. This was on December 6, 1692. William Stoughton was made Chief Justice, with Thomas Danforth, John Richards, Wait Still Winthrop, and Samuel Sewall Associate Judges. At the death of John Richards, Charles Cooke was named to replace him. Whether Sir William Phips, who made these appointments, had detected some special qualities for legal office in these men, or whether the mere fact of their six months' previous service on the bench was the reason, there is no knowing, but the framework of their future careers was determined henceforth. Samuel Sewall would hold the Superior judgeship for the next twenty-five years and after the death of Wait Winthrop be made Chief Justice. During these thirty-six years of judicial service, the title Captain Sewall, by which he had been long known, would be exchanged on official records for his new dignity, but in the thought of many throughout his life, he would con-

tinue to be called Captain, a title that greatly pleased
him. He would still be a merchant and moneylender,
though in reduced volume, and would also divide his
time and thought among his many local interests as before.

His training for the new post was the training of experience, as for his fellow judges on the bench. Not
until after the Revolution was formal legal training
available in America, and in England not until 1758.
In England young men interested in the law gathered
themselves around an older man of law and learned
from him. In America, Tapping Reeve, son-in-law of
Aaron Burr, set up, in 1784, the first American school of
Law in Litchfield, Connecticut.[1] In this school he and
James Gould, his partner and co-instructor, trained
more than a thousand young men before 1820: lawyers,
future senators, cabinet members, judges. During these
years the earlier prejudice against lawyers and legal procedures slowly gave way to eager interest in the law as
a profession. Samuel Sewall would live throughout his
life under the suspicion of law and lawyers which at
times amounted to personal hostility. By his kindly approach, his ability to see the culprit as a human being,
and as he grew older, to temper justice with mercy, he
had a share in overcoming this long prejudice.

His training had begun in the General Court, in
which he had served for seven years before his appointment as judge. Under the original colony charter, the
General and Quarter Courts had exercised, in Thomas
Lechford's word (acid in his tone), "the power of Parliament, King's Bench, Common Pleas, Chancery, High
Commission, Star-Chamber and all the other Courts of
England." [2] He was of course right. Judicial power, not
specifically granted, had been assumed, and all cases of

misdemeanor or criminality had been dealt with at General Court Sessions. For a time during the Andros regime, and briefly afterward, the royal governor had attempted to exercise judicial functions directly, sometimes by the appointment of special courts, as in the witchcraft trials, or by empowering Justices of the Peace to act in legal matters. These arrangements had proved clumsy and had called out wide criticism. The 1692 appointments had been made under provisions of the new charter.

Samuel Sewall had also learned much, as had his brother judges, from the aftermath of the witch trials, particularly as to the nature of evidence and of justice to the condemned. The citizenry had also learned, and court procedures in Massachusetts would be far different from those of the fevered days, June to December, 1692. Sewall was enough of a student to know how to find in print what he needed to know, and he became a regular purchaser of books on the law. In a letter to Thomas Newton, a lawyer of Boston, *en route* to London, he listed for purchase

"All the Statutes at large made since Keble's edition 1684. The Register, Crompton, Bracton Britton, Fieta Miroir, as many of them as you can get in Latin or English, Sir Edward Coke's Reports." [3]

His instruction "as many as you can get in Latin or English" suggests that at least a part of this order was intended for gift or sale instead of for his own private use. A Sewall touch comes in the further instruction, "Let them be well Bound in one or two Covers as shall be most convenient." Always the best, whether he ordered cloth, wine, paper, or books; quality mattered to him.

In the same letter he asks Thomas Newton, "I shall be glad if you would Enquire who it is that signs the Dead Warrant in Capital Cases Tried at the King's Bench, Old Bayly, or before Commissioners of Oyer and Terminer." Such a request, and there are others, supports his own concern for following in detail the patterns of English procedure. This was one of his contributions to New England judicial procedure. He had asked this same question concerning those executed at Old Bailey of Sir William Ashurst, prefacing his inquiry, "There is a matter of Moment in which I want a certainty of Information." His phrase "certainty of Information" is characteristic. Initially, he had lacked much as a man of law, but he knew how to learn.

As a judge of the Superior Court he held court at the time of Sessions in Plymouth, Springfield, Bristol, and Ipswich, riding the circuit in all weathers and being absent from home for several days on each circuit. Usually he went on horseback, as roads in many sections were mere trails and impossible for a chaise. On one attempted chaise journey he "had like to be overset two or 3 times, but God upheld me." [4] Sometimes during Indian uprisings, he journeyed under guard. More than once his horses ran away, wandered from the pasture by night, or were lamed by a fall. His *Diary* reports numerous mishaps which meant further days of delay, sometimes of danger. According to custom, he spent the night wherever darkness overtook him. Nearly all doors were open to travellers in those days and hospitality was as simple as one's everyday fare. Strangers became neighbors on journey, exchanged local news, sang hymns and prayed together, sometimes remaining lifetime friends thereafter. Samuel Sewall's acquaintance throughout the colony was already wide, and the judgeship widened it still further at each session. He often spent a Sunday on circuit, heard a new preacher, perhaps was invited to drive a nail in a new meetinghouse, or to set the tune on Sabbath. Wherever he went, and whatever the errand, he was a churchman, as well as Judge Sewall. Few men in his day outside the pulpit were more conversant with what went on in the meetinghouses of Massachusetts province.

If there were no cases to be heard, the Session would not be held. In a letter to Mr. Partrigg he wrote, "Though would not break away from the Service God and the Province call'd us to; yet we joyfully received so fair a Dismission." [5] This was from the sessions at Springfield in 1700.

The panoply of the judicial office pleased him and it was never omitted. To be met at the county line by the sheriff and gentlemen, conducted to his lodgings, given a parade with fanfare to the court, which would be a meetinghouse or even a private house, if the town had no Town-House, and given "salutation with a trumpet" was never mere routine. In Boston it was salutation by cannon usually, when he stepped on the Artillery Ground on Training Day or over the threshold of the Town-House on the opening day of the General Court. These marks of respect for his office were never omitted from the *Diary* record of the day. Sewall was something of a child in his pleasure from them.

In summer he wore a black silk robe trimmed with white bands; in winter one of scarlet cloth, with wide collar, cuffs and facings of black velvet. One of his gowns worn at the Salem witch trials is still preserved in the Essex Institute memorials. Full length, bright red, flowing, and with a hood, it no doubt added a touch of awe to that far-off meetinghouse drama. His attention to dress and whatever decorum the occasion demanded was punctilious. "Being Artillery day, and Mr. Higginson dead, I put on my Mourning Rapier, and put a black Riband into my little cane," he once wrote. When he presented a pike staff to the Artillery Company in replacement of their borrowed one, it pleased him that "They would needs give me a Volley, in token of their Respect on this occasion. That being so, what matter it will, I suppose, stand me in fourty shillings, beng headed and shod with silver." [6] Such childishness of vanity in a man of his station may perhaps be forgiven. These entries, and there are many of them, help one to imagine his bearing, his measured walk, as he proceeded with slow dignity to the chief place of the assembly, to the foreseat at the Old South on some day of special honor, or even was "accompanied to the Gate" after a private call on an official.

He grew too portly for stateliness after many years, but even with the two hundred and twenty-eight pounds he once recorded, authority walked with him to the bench on Court Sessions. He expected deference and spoke of it as "required to have paid you when you sit as Judge." What sounds like strange vanity may be no more than a strong sense of propriety in line with his office. Once when he was accused of having adjourned the Bristol court somewhat too hastily, he wrote a sharp rejoinder to his critic. It was late in the day, he explained, and the justices had a mile to walk for dinner. The Lieut. Governor had gone on before, and it was "indecent" to make his Honor wait for the Justices of the court. He was a little old-fashioned, no doubt, even in his day with his feeling for ceremony, but his dignity protected him from being ridiculous in his concern for a bow at the right minute as "deference."

Usually the clergy of the area attended Court Sessions, but if not "No Minister being there, I Opened the Court with Prayer." Public prayer was as natural to him as pronouncing a sentence or admonishing a culprit, and he frequently opened and closed the session with it.

Cases handled at these Quarter Sessions were of such sort as human quarrels, disputes, misunderstandings, and tragedies ask the law to settle in any society. "Much business," he often wrote when a session was over. The list of "business" takes us back to the courtroom of a far day: the death plea of a condemned pirate, trespass on another's land, indictment of an Indian girl for firing her master's house, of another for killing her infant child, of a man for riding his horse unmercifully in a storm until it died under him, illegal trading with the enemy in wartime, giving drink to Indians, and always adultery, drunkenness, and assault.[7] The panorama that spreads out before us is of a life as diverse and remote as three centuries, and also as unchanging as the courtroom scene in our own day. Like any other record of early times in New England (or anywhere) it reveals much more than the case in hand on a given day. Crime and punishment are only the framework of the story, the story of a civilization in its early country chapters, a human story belonging to life as it is lived, in any culture, at any date.

Judges in the late seventeenth and early eighteenth centuries had considerable liberty to use their own discretion in the imposing of punishment. Highway robbery might mean only the restitution of stolen goods, or triple restitution, a heavy fine or even imprisonment. Usually, in addition it meant branding with a B on the forehead or in the hand. Adultery, for women, usually meant fifteen stripes "to be laid on her back at the common whipping post." Contempt of his Majesty's government, or false scandalous words against a dignitary meant "to stand in the Pillory or some public place at noon for an hour, wearing on the breast a paper signifying the Crime." The village scene comes alive, as the culprit stands there, taking the rebuke of his fellows who pass by, mocking him, throwing refuse at him, or sometimes sympathizing with him.

Against firm opposition Samuel Sewall stood for several changes in current law. In 1705 he voted against the bill sent in by the Deputies against the marriage of white men with Indians or Negroes. By the provisions of this bill, the colored offender was to be sold out of the Province. "If it be pass'd [Sewall wrote] I fear twill be an oppression provoking to God, and that which will promote Murders and other Abominations. I have got the Indians out of the Bill, and some mitigation for them [the Negroes] left in it, and the clause about their Masters not denying their Marriage." [8]

He also succeeded in adding the clause, "And no master shall unreasonably deny marriage to his negro, with one of the same nation, any law, or custom to the contrary notwithstanding." It is likely that this clemency, particularly toward the Indian, had more to do with his own firm belief, oft stated by him, that the Indians were descended from one of the Ten Tribes of Israel, than with humanitarian feelings toward them, but they profited none the less.

In opposing the death penalty for counterfeiting bills of credit, a very common charge, his arguments were legal rather than humanitarian, and in line with English practice, always important as a guide in his thought.

He was also much pleased with his success, again on the authority of English law, in securing bail for the two young farmers who had refused to turn out of the way for the chariot of Governor Dudley in 1705. Coke's *Statutes* had been the authority he invoked. This sensational case made a great noise in the province, aroused wide interest and deep feeling largely because of the unpopularity of Governor Dudley and, as we look back on it, because also of stiff new attitudes that were beginning to stir in people's hearts. The boldness of these two young countrymen in defying stuffiness (and worse), pleased hundreds who would not yet quite have dared express the same attitude in the presence of the chief executive of the province.

According to the testimony given on both sides, the road was snowy, the Governor's chariot, carrying three passengers and their baggage, was drawn by four horses. An outrider preceded him. The young farmers, John Winchester and Thomas Trowbridge, each had a cart heavily loaded with cordwood. Each side told a different story from this point. In the Governor's testimony, the outrider's order, "Give way to the Governor," was refused, and when given a second time by the Governor himself, John Winchester replied, "I am as good flesh and blood as you; I will not give way; you may goe out of the way." At this point the Governor drew his sword. The young farmer advanced, laid hands on it and broke it.

Thomas Trowbridge, the other young man, told the story differently. Both of the carters had seen the Governor coming and stopped their carts at a point where there were two paths, on one of which John Winchester suggested the Governor could easily pass. At that word the Governor struck the carter's horse, spoke threatening words, stabbed the carter in the back, drawing blood. This was the moment of John Winchester's bold speech and of his hand laid on the sword. Self-defence was his warrant. Each version of the encounter put strong language in the mouth of the other party. "This dog won't turn out of the way for the Governor," Dudley was reported to have said, and when answered by John Winchester with "such words don't become a Christian," replied, "I was a Christian before you were born." A constable arrived at the height of the parley and the two young farmers were arrested.

"What will become of our teams?" one of them asked.

"Let them sink into the soil of the earth," was Dudley's angry retort.[9]

The feeling against Governor Dudley the province over makes it easy to see why this unfortunate episode had stern importance as reports of court action were carried to every corner. At the session of December 14th the battle giving the young men right to have bail was won by Sewall's efforts. He reported his success, "I am glad that I have been instrumental to Open the Prison to these two young men, that they might repair to their wives and children and Occasions; and that might have Liberty to assemble with God's People on the Lord's Day."

Of his last minute record to succeed thus far, he wrote, "I urg'd the words of the Act, that saith regard is to be had to the quality of the person. In publick I offered Coke's pleas of the Crown to be read." The offer had been declined. "I had the Statute Book there, Coke versus Crown, and Reading on the Statutes, stuck to 31 Car. 2nd, that Comands all to be Bail'd that are not Committed for Felony or Treason." [10] Once again, and fortunately for the precedents of New England law that he was building, he was fighting a legal battle, not a human one. This case was before the judges again on a misdemeanor, not a treason charge, and on November 6, 1706, both carters were discharged "by solemn Proclamation." The people had learned something about law as well as behavior through its long progress.

Through the emotional extravagance which had characterized the case on both sides, Samuel Sewall had studiously steered his course searching out English law and precedent for the moderation he might have felt, and then doggedly held to his position through stiff opposition. His contribution to New England legal procedure finds good illustration in this case. The original Code of Liberties in the early colony had been based on the Mosaic law. A Bible verse could determine a case, as in the sad witchcraft trials, "Thou shalt not suffer a witch to live," and nineteen men and women had died on the gallows in 1692, others before them. What he regarded as the law of God as set down in the Mosaic code was never absent from Judge Sewall's thought in his charge to the jury or the framing of a verdict, but he had also applied himself to English law, as in Coke's *Statutes*, and his legal thinking took account of New England heritage as an English colony as well as the seat of God's chosen people in America. His moderation was in line with the thought of his time, but he also helped to establish moderation as legally sound.

Occasionally in his *Diary* he summarizes or quotes from speeches he had made in Court or in the Governor's Council or General Court in Boston. Formal, dignified, definitely patterned, replete with Scripture, a little old-fashioned even for his day, on the printed page they suggest the impressiveness with which they would have been heard. Spoken in full voice in the tenseness of a session, they might have been moving as well as effective for their purpose. The fact that he was the one chosen often to make a salute to a new body of Councillors, who had just taken their oaths, speak the welcome to a new Governor, express honor to one who had died, suggests that his dignity, the formality of his speech, his carefully balanced phrases, nothing too much, nothing left out, were recognized as appropriate for important occasions.

One such occasion was reported after Stephen Dummer had made his speech of acceptance in Council, and oaths had been taken.[11] Sewall wrote, "I stood up and said, If your Honour and this Honourable Board please to give me leave, I would speak a Word or two on this solemn Occasion." His words are those of a man older than seventy, his age at this date, as is also his proud sentence that the Body stood while he spoke and "expressed a handsome Acceptance" of what he had spoken. The occasion was probably typical of the respect his long service and his personal dignity had provided in the respect of his associates. His appeal to the Grand Jury at the first court held in the new Town House, May 5, 1713, was another. "Let never any Judge debauch this Bench."

His speech at Charlestown, January 2, 1717/18, after the death of Wait Winthrop, Chief Justice, would probably have been characteristic of his role as an Elder Statesman at a much younger age. He was then only sixty-two. Facing the empty seat of the Chief Justice he spoke a eulogy, followed by a brief statement of ideals as judge, to jurors, witnesses, ending with the words, "If I have taken up more of the Court's time than is usual, I hope it will be indulged to me, who am the last of the Council left Standing in this Court, of those that have been of it from the beginning." [12] He was prideful of his long service and ambitious to occupy the empty chair of the Chief Justice because of it.

In his letter to Governor Shute, less than a month later, of his willingness to be nominated for this post, he wrote his own recommendation, beginning with a reference to his being "the last of the Justices left standing." Because of the inability of Chief Justice Winthrop to ride the more remote circuits in his turn, he had sometimes presided in his stead.

"And whatever may be objected against me, I presume it cannot be said that I have exercised the Presidency imoderately or Unfairly. And I hope, as the Great Judge (for whose sake I was named) said, I may say, Whose Ox have I taken? And that Partiality or Bribery cannot be laid to my Charge."

He stated also his qualification as the son of Henry Sewall, who was a Gentleman, mentioning also his own considerable estate, and his good health. In twenty years he had been absent from the Bristol court only once from illness. "If I have trespass'd upon the Law of Modesty, it has been to avoid Sullenness." [13]

Much of Samuel Sewall's quality as a man is plain to see from this letter. The duties of the Chief Justice would hardly be different from those he had performed for twenty-five years, but the honor and dignity were deeply coveted. He was also in character when he asked for the nomination directly, and stated his qualifications as he saw them, without false modesty and with full confidence. This was precisely the man his colleagues knew. He was appointed Chief Justice on April 16, 1718, and rode the circuits for ten more years.

The thirty-six years of his judgeship covered his

maturity. They were years rich in experience, and in the work of a country justice, a service well performed. As a member of both the Old Government and the New, he had had a voice in the solving of basic problems. Among these his unceasing battle against the issuing of paper currency called out his best powers of judgment and his stout persistence in a matter of deep conviction. His share in the solution of difficult problems and in the laying of foundations in a time of change from colony to province cannot be fully read in the Archives of Massachusetts. He was a voice at the counsels, at the dinner tables, in the private prayer meetings of the members of the General Court, on the streets of Boston; and in official records we do not hear voices.

Put beside other judges of America in the long file, Samuel Sewall was not a great judge. He lacked the lucidity of mind, the flexibility, which would have enabled him to see a situation from more sides than that of Mosaic law or English precedent. He also lacked the ability to interpret even these standards in principle rather than by letter. He thought literally and applied authority by the letter, trimming his verdict to the measured dimensions of the edict he had summoned in the case. His precision of phrase was one of his best qualifications and served him admirably in argument. Always he acted, as he believed, in God's own sight, searched his own motives and came close to acting as he prayed. No one ever accused him of partiality or self-interest in a decision. On that score he was blameless. Safely enough he could say, "Whose Ox have I taken?"

One reads his resignation in March, 1727, as a record entirely in character. "I went to his Honour the Lieut Governour and desired to lay down my place in the Sup^r Court: I was not capable to do the work, and therefore

was not willing to hold the place. I could not go to
Plimouth Court. I spake now because a gen¹ Council
might be had, and another Judge appointed. His Honᵣ
still desired I would hold; we should hear from England shortly. Mad. Dumer presented me with a very
excellent Orange. Lᵗ Govᵣ thanked me for my Books. I
sent his Honᵣ by Mr. Gerrish Mr. Walter of the Holiness of Heaven, well gilded: to Madam another; To
Mrs. Elithrop Mr. Cooper's sermons. At one a'clock
taken very sick." ¹⁴

In his thirty-six years of service he had dignified
the bench of his day. No contemporary judge more so.

TEN

Phaenomena Quaedam
Apocalyptica ad Aspectum
Novi Orbis configurata

Within the framework of Court Sessions, Council meetings, the General Court, which made his annual calendar of fixed appointments, each with responsibilities to carry throughout the year, Samuel Sewall had another life centering in the Old South Church, in the studies, at the homes and tables of his friends. There were of course excursions to Newbury, to Hogg Island, to Cambridge and various other points, but essentially when he was not riding the judicial circuit, he lived a Boston life. He was a Boston man; in current phrase — "One of the principal men of the Town." He was Judge of Probate, a magistrate, moderating meetings, performing marriages, writing wills, leases, indentures, and unofficially, attending "Treats," calling on friends, acting as bearer at funerals. He also visited the sick, the aged, the dying, the bereaved, prayed with them, read to the blind, and with a regularity of diligence such as they might have expected from their pastor. In addition, he had an intellectual life apart from this daily busyness. He was a considerable reader. He liked good talk about books, and in a very limited way was something of a scholar. Except for occasional items in his *Diary*, record of this intellectual life exists only in the very few published pages from his pen.

In 1697 he published what in his own eyes was his most significant piece of writing, a forty-page tract bearing the ponderous title, *Phaenomena quaedam Apocalyptica ad Aspectum Novi Orbis configurata.* Its text is as coldly removed from the life of his time (or anyone's time) as the title might suggest. Without doubt it would seem to be an extension of his schoolboy tutelage under Thomas Parker of Newbury, who had planted in his mind a durable interest in prophetical speculation and made the book of Revelation a lifelong puzzle. In this tract he is attacking one corner of Thomas Parker's Messianic hope and attempting to prove that North America, in particular the New England portion of it, would be the seat of the New Jerusalem when the Messiah returned to rule his saints on earth. The eagerness of his argument would probably have pleased his not so literal and more learned boyhood teacher, as in the passage,

"The situation of *Jerusalem* is not so Central; but that a voyage may be made from *London,* to *Mexico,* in as little time, as from *London,* to *Jerusalem.* In that respect, if the New World should be made the seat of the *New Jerusalem;* if the City of the Great KING should be set on the Northern side of it; *Englishmen* would meet with no Inconvenience thereby; and they would find this Convenience; that they might visit the Citizens of *New Jerusalem,* and their Countrymen, all under one." [1]

He had been thinking about this subject since he was in his early thirties. In a letter to Cotton Mather in 1684, he had asked urgently, "Please also, in stead of some Recreation, when you can spare the time, to Give me your Reasons why the Heart of America may not be the Seat of the New-jerusalem?" He was still thinking of it nearly thirty years later. In a letter to President Wadsworth of Harvard, "Why isn't N.E. a preface to the [New Jerusalem]? God will as readily Tabernacle in Our Indian Wigwams, as enter into them. What doth signify the most sumptuous and magnificent Buildings of Europe? I hold that He set his Right Foot on the New World and his Left, on the Old." [2] When John Wise "honoured" him with an objection to this view, he wrote, "The only Postulatum therefore that I desire, is that you will grant America an Equal Right with her Sisters in the first verse of the first of Genesis." [3]

On August 22, 1729, five months before his death he wrote Elisha Williams "once more" concerning the new Jerusalem to be built here on earth, before the last day of Judgment.[4] Details of a high mountain which was as the frame of a city (Ezekiel 40, 2) reassured him, and with his characteristic literalness he sought to identify both. The gift of imagination was denied him, but as a jurist searching out cases, he was indefatigable.

The lifelong hope underneath this most ambitious of his writings places Samuel Sewall in one current of the millennial thought of his time, so earnestly dwelt on by older men of the clergy. Other merchants and men of affairs, Harvard trained, would have understood what Sewall was saying and some of them would have shared his hope. He discussed the subject with some of them and often mentioned it in his letters. As was his custom, he distributed this pamphlet widely among his acquaintances. His own familiarity with the materials of theology which it witnesses, and his arguments drawn from these materials, give him some claim to be called scholarly in the clerical manner of his day.

For the modern reader, the hints of what a later day than Sewall's called patriotism are inescapable. His prideful mention of aged Mary Brown of Newbury, still living when he wrote this piece, and, especially, the Plum Island conclusion, one of the most intense pages in all his writing, was penned by a man with a sense of possession no mere deed could convey. Plum Island belonged to him, no spot on earth more so.

"As long as *Plum Island* shall faithfully keep the commanded Post; notwithstanding all the hectoring Words, and hard Blows of the proud and boisterous Ocean; As long as any Salmon, or Sturgeon shall swim in the streams of *Merrimack;* or any Perch or Pickeril, in *Crane Pond;* As long as the Sea-Fowl shall know the Time of their coming, and not neglect seasonably to visit the Places of their Acquaintance; As long as any Cattel shall be fed with the Grass growing in the Medows, which do humbly down themselves before Turkie-Hill; As long as any Sheep shall walk upon *Old Town Hills,* and shall from thence pleasantly look down upon the River *Parker,* and the fruitful *Marishes* lying beneath; As long as any free and harmless Doves shall find a White Oak, or other Tree within the Township, to perch, or feed, or build a careless Nest upon; and shall voluntarily present themselves to perform the office of Gleaners after Barley-Harvest; As long as Nature shall not grow Old and date, but shall constantly remember to give the rows of Indian Corn their education, by Pairs; So long shall Christians be born there; and being first made meet shall from thence be Translated, to be made partakers of the Inheritance of the Saints in Light. Now, seeing the Inhabitants of *Newbury*, and of *New-England* upon the Observance of their Tenure, may expect that their Rich and Gracious Lord will continue & confirm them in the Possession of these invaluable Privileges. *Let us have Grace, whereby we may serve God acceptably with Reverence and godly Fear, for our God is a consuming Fire.* HEB. 12, 28, 29."

ELEVEN

The New England Company

THE 1697 TRACT was dedicated to Sir William Ashurst, head of the New England Company, better known for its later title of Society for the Propagation of the Gospel in New England and Parts Adjacent in America. In his letter of dedication, Samuel Sewall complimented Sir William and also England, "who in shewing Kindness to the Aboriginal Natives of America, may possibly show Kindness to Israelites unaware." For this possibility he was also indebted to Thomas Parker and to various other writers, who held that the American Indians were descended from one of the Ten Tribes. Which tribe and how these descendants found their way to America were the twin puzzles of this theory. Throughout his life Samuel Sewall was concerned to find both answers, and he was by no means alone in his search. Other men of books wrote hundreds of pages on this enigma, particularly as to its geography and the certain identity of the tribe which had fathered the Redskins.

It is not likely that Sir William Ashurst failed to see that in this complimentary dedication Samuel Sewall was placing himself in line for appointment as one of

the American commissioners of the Society which Sir
William headed. The appointment came in 1699. Sewall
was made secretary and one of the commissioners, and
treasurer instead of secretary shortly afterward. He held
these positions until 1721, was deeply interested in the
work for the Indians, and gave generously of his time
in the handling of the Company's funds toward the missionary work among them.

For a New England man to be interested in Indians
was natural enough, and Samuel Sewall had been neighbor to them since his ninth year. It was not as a neighbor
from boyhood, however, that his interest had been
aroused. The center of his concern was that they were
potential converts to Christianity. They were heathen
and he felt something of the sense of mission the first
generation fathers had brought with them in the resolve
to labor toward their conversion. The London Society
which he served, as originally created around a nucleus
of London merchants, had not been primarily a missionary society. Edward Winslow, its originator, in London
during the Massachusetts financial crisis of 1649, had
suggested that funds from certain valuable land properties be expended for missionary work, a cause in which
the mid-century English had keen interest. With John
Eliot as a forceful ally the suggestion had been accepted,
more than a thousand pounds had been spent in New
England in the Indian interest. John Eliot's translation
of the Bible into the Indian language had been printed
with the money, his salary had been paid, and that also
of John Cotton in Plymouth, and of Thomas Mayhew
on Martha's Vineyard.

At the time of Samuel Sewall's appointment as commissioner, there had been many changes in the work of
the Society, mainly brought about by King Philip's War

and the death of John Eliot. William Stoughton, Sewall's immediate predecessor, had had very little interest in the conversion of Indians and funds had been spent otherwise. Sewall began at once to urge the preaching activity.

There was only one meeting of the American commissioners a year, but the handling of moneys to be expended was an all the year responsibility. William Stoughton had employed a clerk for the purpose, but Samuel Sewall undertook the details personally. Claimants for portions of the fund came not only from the missionaries, but from a large number of laymen who performed various small services in or near the Indian settlements. Money from England came not in cash, but in commodities to be transferred from ships to shopkeepers who in time, often a long time, turned over the proceeds to Sewall as treasurer. He entered the expenditures and receipts in books still in existence, a record, which by the names, signatures, and detailed entries is far more than a ledger.[1] To scan these pages is not to wonder at Samuel Sewall's weariness when the time came for his annual report. He acknowledged not being at his best in keeping accounts, giving his wife Hannah the palm, as having "a better faculty than I at managing Affairs." [2]

Far more irksome than balancing the books would have been the very frequent calls at his side door by claimants for funds, merchants with cash from sales, and the equalizing of Company payments with the fluctuating colonial currency. The Company credited according to exchange value as agreed in London, a process entirely familiar to Sewall in his merchandising business. He accepted the tediousness of the detail involved, and during the years of his service as treasurer shaped the

New England expenditures toward preaching and teaching mainly. Tracts were printed on paper sent over by the Society, teachers were trained, and some translations attempted.

One of his more constructive suggestions concerning Indians came in the recommendation that Indian land should have "plain and natural Boundaries, as much as may be; as Lakes, Rivers, Mountains, Rocks, Upon which for any English-men to encroach, should be accounted a Crime. And it will be a vain Attempt for us to offer Heaven to them, if they take up prejudices against us, as if we did grudge them a Living upon their own Earth." [3]

In another letter he argued that such "Lands unoccupied and undesired by the English, may be a valid and lasting evidence, that we desire the conversion and welfare of the Natives, and would by no means extirpate them as the Spaniards did." [4] But always more insistent than this practical suggestion was his zeal in their conversion. On a piece of land inherited from John Hull in Sandwich, he built them a meetinghouse, twenty-four by twenty-eight feet, with two galleries, and to cost thirty pounds. It was to be well-filled between the clapboards and the ceiling with shavings, lest it be cold. [5]

His fairness in all such efforts needs no discounting. One is only surprised to find him once seriously embarrassed when an Indian missionary was sent to his house for the night. There was no way to avoid the necessity of hospitality, which he met by making a bed for him in the study. In his day the physical revulsion felt by white settlers toward the Indian was hardly concealed, and most Boston men in Samuel Sewall's position shared it. One thinks of Roger Williams, a generation earlier, going unarmed into the wigwams of the Narragansetts and Pequods met in negotiations for war or peace, eating with them, sleeping with them, and keeping the peace thereby. Samuel Sewall could not face the essential assumptions basic to the cause in which he labored, at least not in this situation. For all his zeal in their behalf, the root of his interest in Indians was not as men and women, or as individuals, but as descendants of one of the lost tribes.

As such, their conversion from heathenism to Christianity was an obligation he never allowed himself to forget. It was frequent in his thought, in his letters, and once in his attempt at verse. On January 1, 1700, he saluted the new century in "A Prayer, A little before Break-aDay, at Boston of the Massachusetts," as his six-stanza broadside was headed. The third stanza reads,

> "Give the poor Indians Eyes to see
> The Light of Life: and set them free;
> That they Religion may profess,
> Denying all Ungodliness." [6]

TWELVE

'The Selling of Joseph'

O<small>N JUNE</small> 24, 1700, Samuel Sewall published a three-page tract which he called "The Selling of Joseph." This was the first public plea in America against Negro slavery. In his *Diary* five days earlier he had written that he had been "long and much dissatisfied with the Trade of fetching Negros from Guinea and had a strong Inclination to write something about it." He had delayed, until a fourfold reason for doing so had spurred him to take his pen and write this piece.

He lists the four reasons: the reading of Paul Baynes about servants in his *Commentary on Ephesians*, the motion of a Boston Committee for a law to require importers of slaves to pay forty shillings a head, Cotton Mather's forthcoming sheet urging masters to labor for the conversion of their slaves, and at the moment of his long uneasiness about his own delay in writing his protest, the coming of Brother Belknap with a "petition he intended to present in Court for the freeing of a negro and his wife unjustly held in Bondage." By these four reasons Samuel Sewall was led to hope himself "call'd of God to write this Apology for them. Let his Blessing accompany the same."

The petition brought by Brother Belknap may well have been that concerning Adam, the former slave of John Saffin, whose persistent efforts to keep Adam a slave would be in the courts for three years longer. As one of the judges of the Superior Court, Samuel Sewall was directly concerned with this case. A few months later this pamphlet "The Selling of Joseph" would be answered by John Saffin in another pamphlet, entitled "A Brief and Candid Answer to a late Printed Sheet, entitled The Selling of Joseph." [1] The two men were on opposite sides in print as well as in court.

The case of John Saffin versus Adam had begun seven years before with Saffin's promise to release him after this term of service. The Instrument of promise was made legally and bore the date of March 25, 1694. At the end of the seven years Saffin refused the release on the contention that Adam had not fulfilled the conditions upon which the liberty had been promised. In his master's absence, Adam walked off, taking his clothes with him. After a succession of suits, appeals, transfers from one court to another, Adam was eventually freed, but it had been a long tedious struggle. Throughout the various hearings, Samuel Sewall had stood firm as to the illegality of Saffin's action in view of his signed agreement, and also of illegality in his attempt to sit upon his own case, for by various devious moves he had succeeded in being promoted from the bench of the Inferior Court of Common Pleas to that of the Superior Court of Judicature in Bristol, where his case was to be tried. In the end, Governor Dudley refused to commission him as one of the judges.

To later times, the interest of Samuel Sewall's connection with this controversial case in his day is not in its legal aspects so much as in the pamphlet on the larger issue of Negro slavery which it called forth from him. In his own time, thanks to his own wide distribution of it, various contemporaries read it and left some comment, but it made slight impression and brought no visible results. Its interest for later times consists mainly in its date, more than a century and a half before Antislavery became America's issue of the hour. Too early of course to be more than half heard, if heard at all, at the time and sure to be quickly forgotten.

Nothing that Sewall wrote in it is particularly awakening or even original. Nothing that he wrote in it, however, would have needed the merest change to meet the mood of the North in the 1860's, or for that matter of large areas of the world in the 1960's. When thousands were willing to act on the conviction that

"there is no proportion between Twenty Pieces of Silver and LIBERTY,"

so simple an aphorism could be a battle-cry, but in 1700 no one was as yet writing *liberty* in large capital letters as Sewall wrote the word in this short piece. Twenty-five years earlier John Eliot had spoken out against selling Indians as slaves, but no one had as yet pled for Negroes.

In Samuel Sewall's own story this tract is a welcome example of his capacity to be aroused over what he believed to be a current evil, and to use his Bible as a means toward its practical correction. He could be dusty enough in his biblical scholarship, and usually was, but not this time. His title, largely opaque to the average modern reader, would have been clear to the seventeenth century churchgoing man and woman. Along with the three words of his title "Selling of Joseph" would come the picture, familiar since childhood, of Joseph the dreamer, clad in his coat of many colors, wandering in the field, of his jealous brothers seeing him, and when he was come unto them, stripping off his many-colored coat and casting him into the pit. Presently the Midianite merchantmen come by; the brothers pluck him up out of the pit and sell him to the Ishmaelites for twenty pieces of silver.[2]

The preachments drawn from this tale would have been less impressive to seventeenth century readers than the recall of a familiar story, but read against another background, they awaken some surprise, as spoken with ardor in 1700.

"Forasmuch as Liberty is in real value, next unto life, none ought to part with it themselves, or deprive others of it, but upon mature consideration."

"So that Originally and Naturally, there is no such thing as Slavery."

"*Joseph* was rightfully, no more a Slave to his Brethren, than they were to him, and they had no more Authority to *Sell* him than they had to *Slay* him."

"These Ethiopians, as black as they are; seeing they are the Sons and Daughters of the first *Adam;* the brethren and Sisters of the Last A D A M, and the Offspring of G O D; They ought to be treated with a Respect agreeable."

"'Tis Pity there should be more Caution used in buying a Horse, or a little lifeless dust; than there is in purchasing Men and Women."

"And all things considered, it would conduce more to the Welfare of the Province, to have White Servants for a Term of Years, than to have Slaves for Life."

This last suggestion was a seeming practical alternative, but misapplied, since the gaining of effective servants was not the reason for promoting the slave trade. Here was Samuel Sewall, a wealthy merchant, who might have grown wealthier, if he had engaged in importing slaves, inveighing against the less scrupulous of his brother merchants, whose profits were mounting. He speaks as a merchant himself, when he says, "And it may be a question whether all the Benefit received by *Negro* Slaves, will balance the Accompt of Cash laid out for them, and for the Redemption of our enslaved Friends out of Africa." His brother merchants may not have been subscribing, as he was, to the frequent appeals for such redemption. His *Diary* records numerous gifts of money for this cause.

As soon as this little tract was off the press, he began to give it away, as was his custom with whatever he wrote. He gave it to friends, ministers, members of the General Court, some of whom may have felt as he did. Wherever he went, he was well supplied, and all were given away. He was still enclosing copies to his correspondents in 1714, with personal pleas added to "do something toward taking away this wicked practice of slavery. Will be no great progress in Gospellizing till then." [3] A hint that his plea was not entirely obvious comes in a word from Judge Atwood to whom he had sent a copy. "An ingenious Discourse," Atwood replied, perhaps referring to the legal scaffolding of argument. No twentieth century reader would use his adjective.

In a letter to John Higginson, April 13, 1706, Sewall speaks of "Frowns and hard Words" he had met with in the undertaking. [4] The year after it was written, when the Saffin case was in the news, the Representatives to the General Court were instructed "to promote the encouraging of the bringing in of white servants, and to put a period to negroes being slaves." There is no evidence that Sewall's pamphlet was in any way responsible for this suggestion, but there are hints that it did not pass unnoticed.

No wonder. He was striking out against a profitable trade that was growing frightening, even in New England, by the year. There were many Negro slaves in New England at this date, but no reliable evidence that they were well or ill treated. Apparently there was no immediate incentive for arraignment from the pulpit, which was silent on this issue. Sewall was no William Lloyd Garrison, leading a crusade, but he continued to speak out when cases involving Negroes came before him. In 1716, there is a sentence in his *Diary*, "I essay'd June 22, to prevent Indians and Negroes being Rated with Horses and Hogs; but could not prevail." [5]

In a letter to Justice Addington Davenport, who was to try Samuel Smith for killing his Negro in 1719, he wrote,

"The poorest Boys and Girls within this Province, such as are of the lowest condition; whether they be English, or Indians, or Ethiopians. They have the same right to Religion and Life, that the Richest Heirs have." And they who go about to deprive them of this Right, they attempt the bombarding of HEAVEN: and the Shells they throw, will fall down on their own Heads." [6]

Boston Negroes probably knew of his friendly concern. He reports that on New Year's day, 1704/5, "Colonel Hobbey's Negro comes about 8 or 9 *mane* and sends in by David to have leave to give me a Levit [trumpet blast] and wish me a merry New Year. I admitted it; gave him 3 Reals. Sounded very well." [7]

Such a tribute would have pleased Samuel Sewall, as the bows and salutes and occasionally trumpet blasts when he arrived at Court Session. His appeals for Indians at this date won a somewhat warmer response than those for Negroes, but still in limited quarters only.

THIRTEEN

Courtships

HANNAH SEWALL, the wife of nearly forty-two years, died October 19, 1717, aged sixty. Her last illness, written down as "Relapse by a new Cold," was sudden and swift. On Tuesday night her husband and Dr. Oakes sat up with her all night. On Wednesday "The Distemper increased." On Thursday Samuel Sewall stayed home from Lecture, and put up a note asking for prayers. His absence was "taken much note of" as Son Joseph was the preacher, and Son's sermon was seldom missed. On Friday Hannah was still worse, and "exceedingly Restless." Dr. Cutler and Dr. Williams were called. On Saturday Cotton Mather and Benjamin Wadsworth came to pray with her, but she "took little notice." She died a little after four in the afternoon, "whereby the Chamber was fill'd with a Flood of Tears." [1]

On the following day Samuel Sewall attended "publick Worship forenoon and Afternoon" as usual. "My Son has much adoe to read the Note I put up, being overwhelm'd with tears." The funeral on the following Wednesday was attended by the Governor, Boston dignitaries, and the entire General Court, present for the opening of the Session on that day. Sewall gave scarves, rings to the Governor and bearers, and Joseph Allen's sermon, "Alarm to the Unconverted," to the deputies. "Broʳ Gerrish pray'd with us when return'd from the Tomb: I went into it." [2]

No portrait of Hannah Sewall appears ever to have been painted, and little is known of her as an individual woman. She is noted in her husband's diary scores of times, as wife, mother, hostess, companion on a day's journey, riding behind him on a pillion, but usually as mistress of her home on Washington Street. She was the mother of fourteen children, seven sons and seven daughters, of whom only five were living at the time of her death. Daughter Elizabeth, the wife of Grove Hirst, had died in the previous year, and Elizabeth's husband, whom Samuel Sewall called "in a great degree the Stay and Comfort of my Life," died nine days after Hannah's death. In three months' time Sewall was bearer also to three of his wife's bearers. He was greatly bereft by these deaths.

His marriage to Hannah Hull forty-one years and eight months before had brought him wealth as a young man, given him an established merchant business without initial effort of his own, brought him his first public office and by it channeled his career into a long succession of positions of high trust and responsibility. She had satisfied his expectations of marriage, in accordance with the current ideal, and been as he said, his "most constant lover and a most laborious nurse." She missed by only a few months knowing his greatest public honor, the appointment as Chief Justice. He had brought her, throughout their life together, the dignity of a magistrate's home and by his many public services a continuance of the high place socially to which she had been born as the daughter of John Hull. She and her husband had shared a religious faith and a deep concern that their home be built on a frame of piety bearing the first generation stamp. For all these reasons and many more that records do not put down in words, it had been a good marriage.

On February 6, 1717/18, nearly four months after Hannah's death, Samuel Sewall wrote in his *Diary*, "This morning wandering in my mind whether to live a Single or a Married Life." His wandering thoughts need occasion no surprise. That he would marry again was assumed by his friends who were already making suggestions as to the most eligible widows. Sewall himself was watching the foreseat on which they sat in Sunday meeting, and noting the movements of several of them in his entry on adjacent weekdays. New England social custom demanded second and third marriages without delay. Nothing else was expected, and that Samuel Sewall would be obedient to these pressures was taken for granted. In fact, he had already answered his own question before he raised it on February 6th. In his comings and goings about Boston his ears were open to his friends' suggestions for him, to the talk of other courtings by his bereft associates, and to the possibilities presented to his own eyes for changing his state. He had heard that Colonel Byfield was courting Madam Sarah Leverett. Paying a business call on Mr. Willoughby, he was given the hint that "Persons had need be ware how they married again." He replied, "to humor it, They that had been at Sea should be careful how they put to Sea again, especially in winter time; meaning of Old Age." [3]

At this date, Sewall was sixty-six, and beginning to feel the signs of age upon him. On several recent occasions his voice had proved unequal to his praecentor's

duty of setting the tune on Sunday at the Old South.
Accordingly, and no doubt with deep sense of depriva-
tion, he resigned this long honor in which he had taken
delight and pleasure. When his successor White succeeded in setting York tune "to a very good Key" the
next Sunday, Samuel Sewall thanked him and admitted
to himself that it had been "Convenient" for him to resign when he did, his own voice being "enfeebled" by
comparison. Many men of his vocal abilities would have
hung on until asked to resign.

At Roxbury, shortly after the warning from Mr.
Willoughby, and when he was taking an oath of John
Ruggles, he decided he "had not time" to visit Widow
Ruggles. He had been told she was "a very good
woman" and a few days later he inquired of her son
John "How his mother did." At Madam Usher's (on
business) Madam Henchman recommended Madam
Winthrop to him. To enforce this suggestion, Deacon
Marion had come to his house to tell him that "the
Olivers" wished he would "court their Aunt" Madam
Winthrop, widow of Wait Winthrop. "I said little,"
Sewall replied, "twas not five Moneths since I buried
my dear Wife." Mr Leverett told him that he and his
wife had laid out Madam Brown for him, adding that
Madam Winthrop had "done very generously . . . in
giving up her Dower." Obviously Sewall was under
siege. Governor Dudley besieged him still further by
adding that he had laid Madam Winthrop out for him.
Sewall replied that he had already called on her three
times, twice on business. "Cave tertium," Dudley replied, warning him.

Meanwhile, Sewall had written William Denison's
will and on April 7, 1718, had proved it. On occasion of
the proving he was told that Mrs. Denison was "one

of the most dutifull Wives in the World." He began to call on her. Also frequently, "She comes to Our House." He advised with Governor Dudley about her and was encouraged. A few days later "at Our House," he "took her up into my Chamber and discoursed thorouly with her." She desisted somewhat, "desiring me to procure another and a better nurse." He announced he was coming to see her. " 'Twould be talked of," she replied, knowing that there were already watchers. "I answer'd, In such Cases, persons must run the Gantlet." [4]

All seemed to go well for a time. He visited her often. She gave him "very good Curds." He gave her "K. George's Effigies in Coper; and an English Crown of K. Charles 2^d. 1677, and eat Curds with her." On other occasions the gifts were two knives and forks, "Pound of Raisins with proportionable Almonds," a Psalm-Book "neatly bound in England with Turkey-Leather, a pair of Shoe-Buckles, cost 3d." After all these tokens, he told her it was "time to finish our Business." What should he offer her? She did not answer. He replied to his own question by offering her two hundred and fifty pounds a year if it should please God to take him out of the world before her. Apparently she had a price of her own, and she delivered her ultimatum to this unsatisfactory offer, saying she had better "keep as she was, than give a Certainty for an uncertainty. She should pay dear for dwelling at Boston." Asked to make counter-proposals of her own, she refused. Samuel Sewall was nonplussed. When she brought the gifts he had bestowed, he refused to take them. He had been confident of her acceptance of him and expected a "Publishment of their intention next Thursday." Her refusal was a hard blow. He had "yearned" after her, he wrote; "but I think God directs me in his Providence to desist. May

God, who has the pity of a Father, Direct and Help me," he added to the day's entry of his disappointment.

He had now waited a year since Hannah's death, and Mrs. Denison's rejection quickened his determination. He saw her again, when without advance announcement she presented herself at his door on a cold November thirtieth evening at seven o'clock, having come on foot, desiring, as she said, to speak with him alone. Obviously she had been interested in his attentions, and it was his offer made with knowledge of her husband's large estate that had ended it all. "It was hard to part with All and have nothing to bestow on her Kindred." She desired that no one should know she had come to his house on this occasion. Having spoken her mind, she mentioned two glass bottles she had with the other gifts, and being told to keep them, "she went away into the bitter Cold, no Moon being up, to my great pain to see her go." "I saluted her at parting," he wrote.[5] That story was over.

He next tried the widow Tilley and fared better. She had been a guest at his home on January 11th, prior to his courting of Widow Denison. He recorded no every other day succession of visits during the courting, but he probably made them, for on September 19, 1718, he wrote that he spoke with her within her chamber, to "ask her to come and dwell at my house." She was respectful, but felt her "unworthiness." He would have her "consider of it." Three weeks later he gave her a little book that he had once given to "My dear Wife." On Thanksgiving Day his son Joseph married them at Mrs. Tilley's, "in the best room below stairs." The next day Samuel Sewall gave a large party at his home, with "Governor Shute, Governor Dudley and his Lady, Councillors and Ministers, (except I. Mather), Four Tables; Two in the Best Room, Many Coaches here."

This marriage, which seems to have begun satisfactorily, lasted only until May 26, 1719, when his wife died very suddenly. It had been apparent immediately after the wedding that she was not in good health.

As he cast about for the next possibility, something reminded him of Mrs. Ruggles, "my ancient acquaintance and Townswoman" of the far off Newbury days, when he was a schoolboy. She had been Martha Woodbridge, daughter of the Rev. John Woodbridge, and when she was a little girl, he had often met her with her sister Mary, at the end of Mrs. Noyes' Lane, coming from school, each "in their Hanging Sleeves." He recalled all this tenderly, in his letter to her brother.[6] "I could find it in my heart to speak with Mrs. Martha again," he wrote, "now that I my self am reduc'd to Hanging Sleeves."[7] "I could venture to lay my Weary Head in her Lap, if it might be brought to pass upon Honest Conditions," he continued.

The answering letter is not extant, but he apparently received word of her whereabouts, called upon her and in midsummer 1721 presented himself as a suitor. In his word,

"I shew'd my Willingness to renew my old Acquaintance, She express'd her inability to be Serviceable. Gave me Cider to drink. I came home."

The fact that she had been up all night at the birth of a granddaughter may have affected her mood, but two weeks later, when he called again, she made it clear that she would not move out of her house, "till she be carried out," and "Lest it be an obligation on her," she was reluctant to accept the Election sermon that was his token of affection. Samuel Sewall attempted to make excuse for his long stay, as his coach had returned to

Boston with another passenger, and she capitulated to
the extent of saying that she "would be glad to wait on
me till midnight," provided I should solicit her no more.
I said she "was willing to get rid of me." She answered
that was too sharp, and before the coach had returned,
she ended the chapter by accepting the Election sermon
and a two shilling piece for the new grandchild.[8]

His most ardent assault on the widows and the best
known of them all, has been unfairly treated for humor
alone. It is his courting of Madam Winthrop, widow
of Wait Still Winthrop, Chief Justice before Sewall,
and his friend of many years. She was the daughter of
Thomas Brattle, and had been married first to John
Eyre, to whom she had borne twelve children. Samuel
Sewall's approach as a hopeful third husband began
with a request for permission to call upon her. Their conversation on this call was discussion of the seven widows
in the foreseat at the Old South: Rebekah Dudley,
Bridget Usher, Deliverance Legg, Rebekah Loyd,
Lydia Coleman, Elizabeth Bellingham, and Madam
Winthrop herself. She seemed to recommend the widow
Loyd.

On the second call two days later, she kept him waiting. Other callers came, and when they were alone, he
took up the discussion of the widows again, praying that
Katherine might be the one "assigned for me." She in-
stantly denied the indirect proposal, and said she "could
not leave her Children." He prayed her "Consideration," presented her with a sermon, which she put in
her pocket. He "took leave."

He did not wait the week, as agreed, and when he
came again, found her out. He gave Katee, her grandchild, a kiss and a penny, and went to a "Treat" at which
he was given gingerbread and cake to take home. He

preserved the gingerbread and carried it to her the next day, "wrappd in a clean sheet of paper." Again she was not at home, but he waited from 6:00 P.M. until 8:00, fee'd the servants, outstayed other callers, and when he was alone with her confessed that he was "lonesome." "Together we might forward one another in our journey to Canaan." But she was not lonesome, and she repeated her intention not to leave her children. She was courteous, treated him with wine and marmalade, and "I took leave about 9 aclock."

On the following day he sent her by messenger Mayhew's sermon on the state of the Indians at Martha's Vineyard, a letter wishing her a joyful entrance into the two hundred and twenty-ninth year of the discovery of America by Columbus, and hoping he might see her the next day. He found her "full of work" behind her sewing stand, and with countenance much changed, "dark and lowering." She emphasized her reasons for refusing him, but relented to the extent of sending him home with "Juno and a good lantern." He gave her another sermon, one of Dr. Preston's this time. He had been ardent on this occasion, and when she talked of Canary, had replied that "her kisses were to me better than Canary."

After staying away for five days, he found her courteous, but "not in Clean Linen as sometimes." He gave her the day's *Gazette*, and was again lighted home by Juno and the lantern. The next time, finding her out, he followed her to Mr. Walley's where she was calling, and saw her home. She spoke "pretty earnestly" about his keeping a coach, and when he said it would cost him a hundred pounds, she contradicted by saying it would cost no more than forty. He stayed late. On Lecture night she told him he should wear a wig, knowing full

well that wigs were an abomination to him. He went
home to pray with Son Joseph about his floundering
courtship, and called again with a sermon of Dr. Sibbes.
She was out. He waited three hours, and when she returned at 9:00 P.M., he asked when their proceedings
should be published, meaning the banns for the wedding.
She replied that "they were as like to be no more publick
than they were already." At 11:00 he arose to go. She
offered him no wine "that I remember" and did not help
him on with his coat. He asked that Juno light him
home. Madam "open'd the Shutter, said was pretty
light abroad; Juno was weary and had gon to bed." "So
I came hom by Starlight as well as I could."

On a journey to Salem, "in the Hackney coach
through the Comon," he stopped by her house and felt
encouraged by the dram of black cherry brandy she gave
him. He told her: "I was come to inquire whether she
could find it in her heart to leave that House and Neighborhood, and go and dwell with me at the South-end.
I think she said softly, 'Not yet.'" He explained his
position on wigs and a coach, in many words. She wished
him a good journey. On his return he saw her again.
His gift this time was almonds, about half a pound. She
seemed pleased and asked what they cost. These sweet-
meats were of course rare in New England and few had
them. The talk went on to the hundred pounds he would
leave her if he died first. She could have time to "Consider of it." She had looked into the matter herself and
had heard that he had given all to his children by Deed
of Gift. "I told her that was a mistake." She gave him
"a Glass or two of Canary."

At the next call, he arrived before supper and stayed
until her guests departed. What kind of necklace should
he give her? "None at all," she relied. What would she

give him? She "could not Change her Condition." She charged him with insisting that she must put away Juno if she came to him. He denied it. The outcome was of course in sight, but Samuel Sewall was not giving up yet. After more consultation and prayer with his son and his daughter Cooper, he called again. Madam was rocking little Katee in the cradle. She promptly put the cradle between them, and did not eat the remainder of the sugar almonds he presented. "Was she of the same mind as last Friday?" "Thereabouts," she answered, cryptically. "I told her I loved her, and was so fond as to think she loved me. She said she had a great respect for me." He took leave, and as he went down the stair, she "bid me have a care." He had not asked her to remove her glove, as he had sometime done, and he noted that her dress was not so clean as sometime it had been. "Jehovah jireh!" [9]

On the second day after this meeting, he noted that her shutters were open as he passed by at night with a servant and a lantern from Brother Stoddard's. Two days later, he wrote in the *Diary*, "Went not to Mm. Winthrop's This is the second withdraw." He did not call on her again or mention her in the *Diary* until more than a month later, when he heard that she was giving a Treat for her children. He had known nothing of it. He remained in the Council Chamber for fear of the rain and dined alone on "Kelly's pyes and good Beer." Four years later on Lord's Supper Day at the Old South, "Deacon Checkley Deliver'd the Cup first to Madam Winthrop and then gave me a Tankard. Twas a humiliation to me and I think put me to the Blush, to have this injustice done by a Justice." [10]

On March 29, 1722, he married Mary Gibbs, widow of Robert Gibbs, son of a Boston merchant, and the

daughter of Jonathan Shrimpton. His courtship had
been mainly by letter. The bargain she finally accepted
with some compromise was harder than those he had
attempted to drive either with Mrs. Denison or with
Madam Winthrop. Again almonds, cakes, Canary and
sermons were his tokens of interest. According to custom,
he led her into his Pue at the Old South the Sunday after
the wedding, and on the following Sunday they occupied
the foreseat. She survived him.

In June, 1725, five years before his own death, accompanied by his son Joseph, he called on Madam Winthrop in her final illness. She thanked him kindly and inquired "how Madam Sewall did." He said, "I kiss your
hand, Madame." She asked for prayers. After her death
several weeks later, he was one of the bearers at her
funeral. "Will be much miss'd," he wrote in his day's
account.

There is humor of course in the naïveté of this tale,
and would be, if it be translated into the idiom, the
tokens, the social milieu of another day, even our own.
It is the story of a man with youth and the ardor of love
far behind him, a man accustomed to authority and now
a suppliant, lacking discernment for the precariousness
of his situation, pressing his balance-sheet bargain with
a woman far sharper than he in the wisdom of this
world, safe and comfortable in her own independence
and having no wish to change it. Two marriages behind
her, what could she gain by a third? Both man and
woman sat for their portraits as they waged unequal
war, and then remained friends while life permitted.
Katherine Winthrop was not the wife for Samuel Sewall,
nor he the husband for her, as she was wise enough to
know.

One remembers that the story of these courtships was

not intended for our eyes, or anyone's but Sewall's own, and we read it, smile at it, over his shoulder with apology. He took the risk a diary imposes, and has been paid by having his lack of tact, of humor, his business shrewdness, his naïveté, and most of all his utter blindness to see himself caught in his own net written down for what it was, an old man's stumbling attempt at courtship. We feel for him just a hint of pity perhaps, but it is pity chiefly for his blindness and lack of a saving sense of humor.

FOURTEEN

Layman of the Old South

THE CENTER for much of Samuel Sewall's voluntary, unofficial activity throughout his Boston life was Old South Church which he joined in his twenty-fifth year. At that time this third church society of Boston was only nine years old. He remained a member for fifty-three years. Thomas Thacher, the first pastor, had encouraged him to think, when he was a troubled young man fearful to take this important step, that his "stirring up to it was of God," and that he was eligible to become a member. He joined the church on March 30, 1677. Through the remaining year and a half of his ministry, Thomas Thacher continued to be a helpful guide and monitor.

Samuel Willard, who took over as pastor on the death of Thomas Thacher, was only seven years older than Samuel Sewall, and the pastoral relation was strengthened by a close personal friendship between the two men. They were not always in agreement, notably during the witchcraft proceedings, strongly opposed by Samuel Willard, who also, in addition to his outspoken criticism, was said to have helped several of the accused to escape beyond the borders of the colony.

Samuel Sewall asked a great deal of his pastor in terms of personal service, and again and again, particularly when there was illness in the home, the message "Tell Mr. Willard to call God" would be sent in haste to the parsonage. Day or night, he obeyed, coming to the home and staying for hours. A sickroom in those days was a scene of prayer, of brother ministers, together with the pastor, arriving with friends along with the physician. Samuel Sewall had prayed and watched by many deathbeds. It was a service he never refused. Often when a private fast or prayer meeting was held at the Sewall home, Samuel Willard was the preacher, or one of them. He baptized most of Sewall's children and was comforter in the deaths of those who died young. The relation of pastor and church member, especially in the services outside of the pulpit, is detailed on many pages of the *Diary*.

Ebenezer Pemberton, who was first colleague and then became pastor at the death of Samuel Willard, was a man of far different stamp, difficult in his strange outbursts of anger and clearly annoyed at Samuel Sewall's many demands for private service. There were stormy scenes of his "extraordinary Vehemency" [capering with his feet]; as Sewall reported, "I told him he was in a passion. He said he was not in a Passion. I said, it was so much the worse." On another occasion, this entry, "The truth is, I was surpris'd to see myself insulted with such extraordinary Fierceness by my Pastor." [1] Even so, there were quieter times, even prayer and preaching in the home, journeys together, and Pemberton sermons outlined in the Commonplace books. He was an unpredictable man, and Sewall was persistent in his expectation of pastoral attention. Once when he was summoned in an emergency, the pastoral answer came back, "a great deal of Business," and he did not respond to the call.

The relationship became strained when Son Joseph Sewall became a candidate for the office of colleague pastor with Pemberton. On the Sundays during this period, Samuel Sewall listened carefully to see whether the pastor prayed for the younger man, recording in his *Diary* on several occasions, "I did not observe" that he did. On this point Sewall was very sensitive, and he was deeply hurt by the lack of courtesy this omission indicated. But Son Joseph was finally elected and then began one of the happiest periods in his father's churchgoing life. His prideful joy, as he sat in the pew under his son's preaching is not matched elsewhere in his story as a father. Ordination day, September 16, 1713, was a great day in his life. He writes the record with enthusiasm. There "was a very great Assembly." Cotton Mather had begun with prayer, a little after ten and "concluded about the Bell ringing for Eleven." "My son preached from I Cor. 3.7." There were elders and messengers from nine churches of Boston and the Bay. "Twelve Ministers sat at the Table by the Pulpit. Mr. Pemberton made an August Speech, Shewing the Validity and Antiquity of New English Ordinations," and when he had finished, asked the customary question, had anyone anything to say "against ordaining the person?" No one spoke in criticism. Mr. Pemberton "took the Churches Handy vote; Church sat in the Gallery." Four ministers "laid on Hands," after which "Mr. Pemberton Pray'd, Ordain'd, and gave the Charge Excellently. Then Dr. Increase Mather, made a notable Speech, gave the Right Hand of Fellowship, and pray'd." All sang the twenty-third Psalm, after which "the person now Ordain'd dismissed the Congregation with Blessing." There was of course considerable entertainment afterward, at Mr. Pemberton's chiefly; "Two Tables at our House." A great day indeed.[2]

In his *Diary* accounts of Joseph's preaching thereafter, he writes his name the "Rev. Mr. Sewall" almost always. From such of his sermons as have been printed, he cannot be called an extraordinary preacher, but in his father's ears his sermons were heard and set down in the record in the worthiest terms. Father and son enjoyed a close relationship, even from Joseph's early years, and the relationship deepened as they grew older. They prayed together very often and always talked over their anxieties and their decisions together. Son Joseph performed his father's second wedding ceremony. Perhaps something Samuel Sewall had missed in turning away from the pulpit himself was satisfied in his son's ministry.

Ebenezer Pemberton preached his last sermon on January 20, 1717/18, and Joseph Sewall, then aged only thirty, was pastor thereafter. In October of the same year, in accordance with the custom of the church, Thomas Prince was ordained as his colleague. It would be forty years before the Old South witnessed another ordination.

Rather strangely, Samuel Sewall was never made a deacon of the church. His chief office was that of precentor, a service which he performed with deep pleasure for twenty-four years until, one by one, he began to lose what he called his "organs of music, both upper and lower." His *Diary* contains many references to setting the tunes, York, St. David's, Windsor, Oxford, again and again, often finding something individual to say about the singing under his leadership. His responsibility was never routine to him. After his sixty-sixth year, his voice began to be, in his own description, somewhat "enfeebled," and he failed sometimes to set the tune satisfactorily. Once he reported intending Windsor, but falling "into High Dutch, and then essaying to set another Tune," and going into "a Key much too high." Again he "set York," but the congregation went out of it into St. David's, in the second going over. "They did the same three weeks before." "This seems to me an intimation and call for me to resign the Praecentor's Place to a better Voice." He persisted in his resolve, in spite of being urged to continue. "I think it was Convenient that I had resign'd, being for the benefit of the Congregation," he wrote.[3]

Examples of his pleasure in music are frequent throughout his life. It was to him a natural form of self-expression. One of the most touching of these examples was recorded on the day of his mother's funeral in Newbury. This was in mid-January 1700/01. As he wrote the record, "I followed the bier single," and when he saw "Nathan[1] Bricket taking in hand to fill the grave," Sewall said, "Forbear a little," spoke a quiet tribute to the mother of the six sons and daughters who stood by, and "made a motion with my hand for the filling of the grave. I could hardly speak for passion and Tears." [4] That evening the "Two Brothers and four sisters being together, we took Leave by singing of the 90th Psalm, from the 8th to the 15th verse inclusively." Fitting indeed, and in the spirit of their whole lives, childhood and maturity together.

To read the hundreds of *Diary* items concerning sermons, prayer and fasting, both public and private, family devotions, conscientious keeping of Sunday, Bible reading for devotion, one cannot escape the recognition that

religion was very near the center of Samuel Sewall's
way of life and of the meaning of life as he understood
it. One treads softly in trying to discover the bounds and
limits of that meaning for anyone, and for a seventeenth
century man, perhaps it is not to be discovered by those
to whom the certainty of approved doctrine is not absolute or the Bible the dictated word of God Himself.
Perhaps the answer is best to be found in the sermons
for which Sewall wrote down the text and doctrine so
confidently. God's world in these sermons is an ordered
world, its symmetry perfect. Man has grievously sinned,
but reconciliation with God is still possible through
God's own plan for redemption. Any child in the Old
South congregation could have told what the *covenant*
meant to those who listened on any Sunday morning.
Once Samuel Sewall spoke of "bursting into tears" at the
thought of Christ's blood shed for him. Read any hundred of these sermons for their dominant themes, and
many things become clearer.

Religion to Sewall spelled certainty, absolute and
complete, a condition of mind rare indeed to modern
men of thought. Samuel Sewall was not a man of
thought. He was not tortured by unanswered questions,
but comfortable in what he called belief. The literalness
of his mental processes might seem childish to later
readers. Simple certainly, they were; perhaps not childish. "I hope God heard," he once wrote after a session
of prayer with Joseph, grown man. That such literal
confidence in prayer comforted and reassured him has
frequent record. "To ease my burdened mind in prayer,"
he would say, and the ease came. To turn the points of
the sermon into petition, as he reports doing, for an hour
in a quiet spot would stretch a man's mind and perhaps

carry him out of himself. Prayer was an exercise of religion and quieted his spirit. Perhaps it made him less
self-centered and more humble.

Prayer had been an important element in the Sewall
home and in the guidance of the children. When daughter Betty, aged fourteen, had been "wounded" by her
father's reading of a sermon the week before on the text
"Ye shall seek me and shall not find me," she had been
frightened, had felt unforgiven and in line for "hell."
Her father sent for Samuel Willard, who "prayed excellently" with her. Sewall also "prayed alone" with
her, and with all his children.[5] The notable "piety"
spoken of in his own day probably owed something to
these same exercises of religion in which he had been
trained as a small boy, as in *Diary* examples.

"Even a family is a little Kingdom," he had once
written in annotation of a motto he was sending to his
daughter Rebecca, and in the kingdom of his own home,
religion had been the cornerstone. His words to bring it
about were sometimes pompous, but the fervent wish
that his children "speak the Language of Canaan naturally and well," was utterly direct. His way of bringing
such a result about owes much to the painful pieties of
eight year, eleven month Elizabeth Butcher, whose
parents were members of the Old South. After Elizabeth's death, Joseph Sewall had written the Preface.
The account of the pieties in Samuel Sewall's children
should be read with the accent in mind on early anguish
for sin which had called forth these exhibitions, and the
earlier ones resulting from Dr. Janeway's *Token* [6] and
Cotton Mather's imitation of it in his *Token for the
Children of New England*, as well as in *Early Piety,
Exemplified in Elizabeth Butcher of Boston*, not published until 1718. Sewall was following a mode, not

creating one, when he taught little Judith, aged three
and ill, to say after her father, "Create in me a clean
heart, O God and renew a right spirit within me." She
must be ready to go when her time came, as was un-
happily too soon. She was his last child, whose birth
coming in his own fiftieth year had made it "a jubilee"
to him. He honored a child's exaggerated distress for
sin (parentally induced) not by trying to put it out of
the child's mind, but by dealing seriously with it. Examples are plentiful, and to spare. The *Diary* offers
many in the early years of his children's lives.

As the years went on, many changes came and swiftly.
Of his fourteen children, only five were left when his
wife Hannah died in 1717. One after another, he attended the funerals of his Harvard classmates, until
only Edward Taylor of Westfield, his college chum and
bedfellow for two years and his correspondent for life
thereafter was left. He too would slip away before
Samuel Sewall. Many of the pews of his fellow worshippers at the Old South were now occupied on Sunday
by a younger generation, whom he scarcely knew. He
had attended the funerals of the older ones and carefully
recorded them in his *Diary*. When the church issued its
Historical Catalogue [7] a century and a half later, these
items supplied the only information about some of these
earlier members. Many pages in the *Catalogue* reprint
what Sewall had written; otherwise some of these men
and women would have no record, their tombstones having long ago crumbled.

Samuel Sewall began to speak occasionally in his day's
record of his own infirmities. He gave up the long horseback rides, the Harvard Commencements, many of the
"Treats," the frequent calls on so many of his Boston
friends, and began to live a less active life. "I am moul-

dring down, as my Uncle Quincy's phrase was," he wrote
to Nehemiah Walter in late summer, 1726.[8] He had
been re-elected to the Governor's Council in 1725, but
had declined to serve. "I being a lame and fainting
Soldier, they would be troubled to carry me on their
shoulders. Would be better without me," [9] he told the
committee who came to his home to try to persuade him
to serve again. He could not be persuaded and sent his
letter of resignation on June 4, 1725.[10] He had been
elected thirty-three times and had outlived all those
originally selected in 1692.

In 1728 he also resigned from the post of Chief
Justice, as he had tried to do in the preceding year. "I
was not capable to do the work," he wrote in his *Diary*
entry for March 11, 1726/27, "and therefore was not
willing to hold the place." [11] He also resigned as Judge
of Probate in 1728.

After the severe earthquake of 1727, Old South
church building needed repair. A committee was appointed to "view the house and consider what is needful
to be done towards the repairing of it, and the charge."
The committee came back with a recommendation for
two committees, one to see what to encourage toward
repairing the building, and another to see what to encourage toward rebuilding it. Reports of both committees were heard on February 25, 1728, and on February
27 the question was put to the brethren.

Samuel Sewall was firmly against rebuilding. It is
easy to see why. There was no building in Boston, aside
from his own home, which had been more precious to
him. The Town-House had burned in 1711, and there
had been time to become accustomed to the new building. He would not have time enough left for a new Old
South to be other than new to him. His own religious

life, and the history of his family was bound up in the old building. John Hull had been one of the founders. With Hannah, his wife, he had worshipped there in all their forty-two years of married life. His children had been baptized there. He could not vote to destroy it. He spoke out strongly in disapproval, and when he was out-voted, forty-one to twenty, he asked only that his adverse vote be put in the record, and henceforth he kept silent. This was entirely in line with his lifelong practice in General Court or Governor's Council.

In his letter to the Pastors and Brethren, February 20, 1727/28, he gave his reasons for opposing the re-building. It was unseasonable. The old building was a good meetinghouse. There was not room to build a new structure while the old one stood. Where would we worship while the new structure is "setting up?" "Upon these, & such like Considerations, I dissent . . . and pray that what I have written may be entered in the Church Records." It was so entered [12] not in the Records, but in the *History of the Old South Church*.

He would not worship in the new structure he had opposed. Death came gently on January 1, 1729/30. He was in his seventy-eighth year, and would have been seventy-eight on March 28th. He had been enfeebled for something more than a year, with periods of illness that had kept him away from service on occasional Sunday mornings. The congregation was worshipping in the Old Brick during the rebuilding. His final illness was only a little more than a month long, and had not been especially painful. He merely grew weaker by the day. His son Joseph left a few details in his own *Diary* [13] especially of his father's religious exercise. He repeated the creed and the Lord's Prayer, was entirely calm and spoke very little.

The funeral was held on January 7, with burial in the Hull tomb in the Old Granary Burying Ground, where Father and Mother Hull, his wife Hannah, and so many of their children were lying. Thomas Prince preached the funeral sermon on the text, I Samuel 7, 15–17, beginning, "And Samuel judged Israel all the days of his life." Joseph Sewall preached another sermon *The Orphan's Best Legacy,* from the text Psalms 27, 10, "When my Father and my Mother forsake me, then the Lord will take me up." [14]

There was no will. His estate was settled by his two sons, Samuel and Joseph, and Mr. Cooper, the husband of his one surviving daughter. The Mansion House, as Samuel Sewall had rebuilt it, was given to his son Samuel, who took up his residence there.

FIFTEEN

The Diary

SAMUEL SEWALL'S most significant legacy to the American generations after him has been his *Diary*. Kept from December 3, 1673, to October 13, 1729, it covers nearly fifty-six years, with a gap of seven years for the lost volume from March, 1677, to February 11, 1684/5. The first entry is in his twenty-first year, before he had taken his second degree at Harvard; the last, a little more than two months before his death.

In these pages of day to day record, the last quarter of the seventeenth century and the first quarter of the eighteenth take on the color and accent of life. Boston becomes a community of some five or six thousand men and women living a corporate life. There are as yet no heroes. All are on the level of today. Magistrates, some of whose names history remembers, meet at the Town-House, transact the day's business, treat each other at their homes or in the Council Chamber, hear sermons on Sunday or at Thursday lecture, sing, fast, drink together. As men of affairs they acquire a new dimension and lose most of their dressed-up importance. Ministers have a six-day secular life as well as a pulpit authority; sometimes they go fishing. Shopkeepers, merchants, ap-

prentices and other lesser folk are their neighbors, as
well as their parishioners. They talk of their common,
shared, weekday interests, as well as of their souls' sal-
vation. The sons and daughters of one social stratum
marry the sons and daughters of another. The Artillery
Company trains, drums beat and trumpets sound; ships
arrive with much fanfare, and in time weigh anchor and
depart. Offenders are carried to the meetinghouse in
chains to hear their last sermon before they are carted
past to execution, everyone following. Indian scalpings,
disease, "vehement weather" bring disaster. There are
funerals on every page. Many children do not live
through their first week, but all have been baptized on
their first Sunday. Year by year in its season, snow falls,
and at mid-April, "the swallows announce the spring."
A composite life unrolls, thickly interwoven, often
tangled, simultaneous, written down as it happened, and
without evaluation.

Samuel Sewall, by whose patient industry these pages
are ours to read, was one man in this crowded story.
Readers come to know him by what he chooses to report,
for this is not an autobiography. It is the objective record
of a provincial town, and a relatively small one during
one man's half-century as its self-appointed scribe. The
entries are of the almanac variety, except that the re-
corder has more than one line to fill for each day. Almost
unvaryingly, he writes as if in answer to the question,
What happened today? Facts, not experiences; opinions
seldom; interpretations hardly ever. This is an objective
story.

Unlike the greater English diaries of his day, John
Evelyn's, Simon D'Ewes', most of all, of Samuel Pepys',
Sewall's record is not a major, hardly even a minor
source of history in his time. History gains, however,

by his tale, not in fact, hardly obscure fact often, but in reflected attitudes, motives, loyalties unrevealed in documents of state. Why did New England officialdom behave so seeming childishly over the cross in the colors, for example, or how can one understand the intolerance, the lack of graciousness in forbidding a Church of England service in a Boston meetinghouse? To read Samuel Sewall's entries, not on one day, but through weeks, is to sense the anger, the superstition, the loyalty to something their own which was already old enough to be revered. The Andros revolution set down in the report of action on the streets and in Council is a bare shell without the behind-the-scenes manifestations official records do not report. Similarly the Navigation Acts, in terms of visible disobedience to them, the persistent pleas for restoration of the lost charter, in the fact alone, are less than half the story.

One reads of these backstage repercussions in these pages, not as finished fact, but as process moving toward fact, through clamor at the Town-House, heat in Council meeting, repressed anger in public and an explosion in private, in days of fasting and prayer for God's help, in the slow birth of a new idea, in one man's voice at the right time in the right place, and maybe his name is forgotten. Samuel Sewall's dry question, when a formal petition was to go to the King, requesting a new charter for Harvard, "Whose college is it? I asked," Not a question at all, and it tells us something which should not have been forgotten when tomorrows came.

How true are these recorded attitudes, motives, loyalties? How individual? How general? There is no uniform answer. One moment, one day only is being recorded. These are immediate impressions; not considered judgments. They are one man's vision of one

day's happenings. Clear? Blurred? Certainly, sometimes
one, sometimes another, as in all our seeing.

Why did Samuel Sewall write these many hundred
pages? Not a difficult question. He wrote from the same
impulse that impelled New England men from the
earliest days to enter on the almanac pages for each day
of the month what they could write on the one line for
each day of that month. Extant almanacs that hung by
the fireplace in every colonial household from the first
year of their publication preserve the story. There are
hundreds of items that tell more than they say, as

Today the red cow calved.
Stephen was born today.
Great snow. Thin meeting.
This day died my wife.
Smallpox comes.
This day a bluebird sang.
The Lord is my Shepherd.[1]

Scrawled in pencil, perhaps at bedtime, on these pages
which some chance has preserved, the almanac record
takes one back within the four walls of another century.
The record is stark, clipped in its finality, but much
comes with it, unwritten. It is a human story, a family
story, of hardship, courage, sorrow, faith, persistence,
sometimes of beauty and hope. Ministerial diaries or
journals of these days furnish fuller records of parish
and town. Without such of them as have come down to
us, many pages of a town's early history would be blank,
scores of first settlers would have no names. The urge
to write it all down as it happened was not questioned or
analyzed; it was only obeyed. Samuel Sewall was heir
to this long custom, and he obeyed it also.

Whether he revised his record or not, he does not say,

but the evidence of the *Diary* page would seem to be against revision. The preservation of a few almanac pages and their correspondence to the *Diary* entry, sometimes with slight expansion, sometimes reduction, suggest that on journey he probably took notes for later entry.[2] The *Diary* is too large a book to have been carried with him.

Apparently he kept no diary during his Harvard days, as some students were doing. Such student records in his day were usually of personal religious experiences, and kept for short times only. His Harvard residence was nearly over when he made his first entry. It is highly likely that the example of John Hull, at whose home he is thought to have lived for a time in 1674, may have had much to do with his embarking upon keeping a diary likewise.

John Hull's *Diary* [3] concerns his own affairs mainly, his shipping successes or failures, and his pious acceptance of both. One gets the impression of a righteous man, with a clear-cut personality. He reports no trivialities, leaves no blurred edges, sees everything in clear black or white. His word can be trusted, his conduct predicted as blameless according to the Ten Commandments. No entry could be exchanged with one from Samuel Sewall without immediate detection. Objective as both diaries are, each belongs to the man who held the pen. By the same test neither could entries from Sewall be exchanged with those in diaries of men in his own time and experience. Allowing for the difference in material out of which the entries are made, Sewall's diary as compared with the greater one of Samuel Pepys reports events without his own involvement in them. Pepys is deeply involved in what he reports. There are many other fundamental differences.

Samuel Sewall's choice of details and his direct statement of them, almost as in conversation, is established in
the earliest pages. The items are mainly local, the range
wide, the trivial in uncounted wealth, unsorted minutiae,
jostling one another incongruously on every page. It is
a gossipy story without reflection, but with unconscious
overtones. From his first pages:

I had my hair cut by G. Barret.
It thundered and lightened and rained very much.
Tobacco pipes 3d.
Received my Quarter pay; borrowed money subducted.
There were this day two boyes killed at Watertown with
    the tumbling of a load of brush on them, on which they
    road: the one was about the age of 12 years, and the
    other 9.
One shilling to my brother.
My little Neece Born.[4]

We shall have such items by the hundred: news of
family, college, colony, significant events and small talk.
It will also be a book of people. Who were born? Baptized? Who are ill? Who died? Who courted and who
married? Who bore the corpse and in what order? Were
there scarves, gloves, rings? Who preached and what
was the text? Who were offenders? What did they do,
and what was the punishment? Open a volume of the
Diary anywhere, and from snippets a story emerges.
The genealogist will neglect these pages to his loss.
Hardly a page does not have a dozen early Boston
names. Put the entries together and we know much
about these men and women before the year is over.

Repetition is part of any such story, and without it,
something of the quality of the story is lost. To collect
what are called typical items from various pages and

print them sparingly as samples result in a quite different book. There are new connotations with each repetition. To report a cold day at Sunday meeting in January
would not be news, but to write,

"This day so cold that the Sacramental Bread is frozen
pretty hard, and rattles sadly as broken into the Plates," [5]

makes it a particular day and a very cold one indeed. We
fill out the item with discomfort in the pews and for a
two-hour sermon to shiver through. On another cold
January day,

"At six a'clock my Ink freezes so that I can hardly write by
a good fire in my Wives Chamber." [6]

His manuscript page shows a less legible hand, in testimony to the stiffness. Yet at meeting that morning
"Though twas so cold, yet John Tuckerman was baptized." He was probably less than a week old.

Sometimes a weather item becomes a full picture. The
Governor and his Lady are crossing the river from
Cambridge on the ice. Their sleigh has four horses with
Troopers riding ahead. The ice breaks and all four horses
and the two Troopers are thrown into the water. The
two horses nearest the sleigh, borne down by its weight,
are drowned. Men run with ropes, planks in rescue.
There is shouting, confusion and a crowd assembling.
When the drowned horses are drawn forth on the solid
ice, it is "A sad Spectacle indeed." In clipped details,
the story has fulness. In another similar mishap, when
the sleigh overturns, the horses run away with the
foundation, leaving the occupants sprawling in the snow.
The fact that the Governor loses his wig, though trivial
enough, is not unimportant to the picture.

In 1687, when the British sent a fleet of ships to take

great tree trunks for ship masts, Sewall reported a picture that will have no parallel in later New England life. He wrote,

"Ride into Swamp to see a Mast drawn of about 26 Inches or 28; about two and thirty yoke of Oxen before, and about four yoke by the side of the Mast, between the fore and hinder wheels. 'Twas a very notable sight." [7]

Fires give him a chance for many pictures of confusion, tragedy, and the kindness of neighbors. The alarm comes during preaching; everyone rushes out, making great disturbance. It is only a chimney fire. Sometimes it is a "dreadfull Fire," with "Two hundred and Sixty odd Pounds gathered at the South Church, the oldest Meeting House in Town," to help those who have lost all. This fire could be seen "20 Leagues off." [8] Sewall himself had lost a house in this fire, but not his own residence. Cotton Mather "improved the occasion" by a sermon entitled, "Burnings Bewayled." "Have not Burdens been carried through the Streets on the Sabbath Day? Have not Bakers, Carpenters and other Tradesmen been employed in Servile Works on the Sabbath Day? When I saw this . . . my heart said, Will not the Lord for this Kindle a Fire in Boston?" Discovery that the fire had been set did not disturb the preacher's confidence in God's way of getting even.

One of the most frequent items in every week of the year is the funeral. All are the same, all are different, each with a picture that stays in the eye. Of the funeral for Peter Thacher,

"I rode in my coach to the Burying place, not being able to get nearer by reason of the many Horses." [9]

It is a seventeenth century scene no one has sketched for us. There is also one of snowy ways made difficult by the carts, wagons, sleighs, bringing cordwood to Boston. On Christmas Day, 1711, (as always, he calls it December 25th) "We had much ado to get along for the multitude of Sleds coming to Town and returning." Once on "a new Rode" he "rid near 14 miles without a house." [10]

At the execution of John Welch, Captain of the briganteen, and six of his accomplices, "the River was cover'd with People, I was amazed. Some say there were 100 Boats. 150 Boats and Canoes, saith Cousin Moody of York."

"When the scaffold was hoisted to a due height, the seven Malefactors went up. Mr. Mather pray'd for them, standing upon the Boat. Ropes were all fasten'd to the Gallows (save King, who was Repriev'd). When the Scaffold was let to sink, there was such a Screech of the Women that my wife heard it sitting in our Entry next the Orchard, and was much surprised at it. Our house is a full mile from the place." [11]

We are at another "vast Assembly, and the street full of such as could not get in." It is at the Old South where Sarah Threeneedles is carried to hear her last sermon. She was executed the next day, "vehement" to the end. Her story needs no heightening of the imagination. Told in fact, literal fact, as seventeenth century eyes saw it, it has a long foreground, and does not end at the gallows.

Had Samuel Sewall picked out what seemed to him important from the day's happenings, we might have missed the best value of his pages. Instead, in this unsorted, unappraised assortment, we are made partakers of the common life in its everyday reality. We come to know by being present many times the wedding customs with their "cake, musick, cheese" afterward; of funerals, invitational by the gift of gloves, rings, scarves; of infant baptism, the child carried by the midwife and lifted

up by the father, the new mother's later party for her
midwives; the protocol of town meetings, governor's
Council, court session, with always the precedence of
ministers, walking ahead of civil officers, and the consternation when it is overlooked. The Rev. Mr. Pemberton was angry because no one accompanied him to the
door. Men go from house to house visiting their friends
who have smallpox, house builders quarry their foundation stone from the Common, fully ten quarts of
Madeira are needed to raise a barn. Bedtime is at nine,
and one carries a lantern to light him home in the dark
streets. The watch goes forth at 11:00 to quell dis-
turbances and returns at 5:00 A.M. Ninepins played on
Mt. Whoredom (Beacon Hill) is one of these. There is
stormy protest against "voting by Papers" instead of by
full-throated *Ayes* and *Nays* as from the beginning.
Cotton Mather's maid gives birth to a child and he turns
her into the street. We are told none of this for information. It is presented without comment. We look on.

An autobiography that views long areas of life in
perspective would use little of all this circumstantial
detail which makes Boston live so vividly in our eyes.
The years to the fixed point of recall would have over-
laid most of it deeply. That which was not seen at the
moment and perhaps not even dreamed in earlier times
would be the autobiographer's story. He would be telling us what only he could know, as Samuel Sewall almost never does. The diarist is at home just after the
fire, the runaway, the execution, the funeral, the insult
at town meeting. The confusion is still in his ears. Sewall
was not writing, as Amiel said, "A legacy of his own
mind and heart." He was writing the daily life of the
common world, surface Boston, as he saw it.

Had he any thought that other eyes than his would

ever read what he had written? An inevitable question about any such record, and in fairness to him, unanswerable. From the apparent unconsciousness of an audience, often the telling of what he might not want anyone to know of his own poor figure in some situation, one would say no. With the exception of entering the almanac pages at some time later than the event, there would seem also to have been neither revision nor preparation for publication. He wrote as many other men of his time were doing, for the record only. Did he read over what he had written and enjoy it? For record of the sermons heard long before, yes, occasionally, and reports being sometimes "comforted" by them.

As one lays the books down, another question. What kind of man comes through these many pages? A man with so sharp a sense of fact that in what was probably often a hasty first draft, he gave the fact edges and colors, measure and movement under his pen. It is the fact as eyes see and ears hear it, external, tangible. Samuel Sewall was incapable of introspection. The Augustinian sense of autobiography as a "man's search for his own true self" is life on another planet as compared with this record. It is not a book of experiences, in which facts become almost symbolic; it is naked fact itself. When Samuel Sewall was off on circuit on his birthday, he went into a meetinghouse alone for private prayer. At home on this occasion, he drew the shades and for nearly the whole day, fasted and prayed. He tells us on one occasion what he prayed for. The minister's hour or one and a half hour prayer at the Sunday service was his model. He prayed by catalogue, until the world, its battles, its woes, its eternal hopes had one by one been carried afresh to God's ears. If in these periods of prayer Sewall had tried to find himself, he would have counted over the duties he owed and matched them in his own performance. One does not know another's spirit, but so it would seem in these *Diary* pages of which his own religion is in some way the subject. Sermons, "Excellent"; prayers, "Excellent"; it was his favorite adjective for an acceptable Sunday performance. He used words precisely, and *excellent,* so frequent in this connection, no doubt had a specific meaning.

Aside from such self-revelation as comes in the many passages about religion, Sewall seems to see himself as one of the "principal men of Boston" in his later life, seldom absent from his seat at the Council, or the Court circuit, conscientious always, as was entirely true. To see the self-importance and self-approval apparent in his very bearing as he walked the streets, his confidence in his own safe orthodoxy, was not his talent. Had he attempted to write an autobiography, he would not have revealed these qualities so plainly as he does in the objective story, in which it is often an unconscious undertone.

It is the *Diary* as the record of a chapter in New England living which makes it one of the most valuable books preserved to us from the period it covers. It is a treasure house for the social historian, a human document of immense importance in a nation's history. It is also so personal a book that after a hundred pages, or less, a door opens into an earlier America, and one hears a man speaking.

EPILOGUE

WALKING DAILY before his contemporaries through the half-century of his Boston residence, Samuel Sewall appeared to them as a man who stood for the old faith, the old ways, already different enough from current thought and ways to seem a little old-fashioned. His wealth also, his prominence in so many currents of Boston life removed him a little from the levels on which the many walked. A man's life was not yet partitioned off into single corners, but Sewall could be at home in more corners than most men of his day. He stood a little apart from the many, but as he passed in the street, most Boston men recognized him, and gave him a slight bow, as they might not do to each other.

Whittier's imagination was probably correct when he wrote, "stately and Slow" his gait; not just the gait of a man of affairs or a business man, for Boston was beginning to walk faster. Perhaps another reason to justify Whittier's adjective was the two hundred and twenty-eight pounds weight which Sewall reported late in life. But dignity was with him lifelong, whatever his weight. Doubtless even in the young scene on the Common, when his horse, frightened by the militia in training, ran away under him. He took off his hat (always a precious possession), held it tightly under his arm, let the horse go at full speed, and kept his seat. He would keep it through life, whatever the emergency. Even in dissent or in mild anger (rage was impossible to him) in Council or on the bench, his dignity was always adequate to the strain.

Some of what seemed a little old-fashioned to his younger contemporaries were mere crotchets, and he had his full share of them: his many words, public and private, on the abomination of wigs, and instead, the black silk cap and the long white hair; his aversion to Christmas, and his outspoken pleasure when he saw the open shops, the people trading, the carts laden with cordwood coming to town on "the 25th of December"; his mountainous scorn when the minister said St. John, St. Mark, St. Matthew; why not St. Moses as well? Crotchets all, trifling and easily forgiven.

What his younger contemporaries did not see was that Samuel Sewall was more a man of ongoing Boston in his day than a defender of what had been left behind. He saw the changes, protested some of them, but went along with more than he protested. He was part of the prosperity his younger associates were enjoying, and his tight business ways had taught some of them how to succeed also. What gives a certain uniqueness to the figure he cut on Boston streets as one of the "chief men of his day" was that he was both old and new. He was not shedding "Old Man's Tears" for a lost Eden, nor taking on the ways of the Cavaliers. New England was not a lost world to him. " 'Twill be extream hard for you to find so good a Country," he wrote to one of his English correspondents late in his life. His sense of what the Fathers had done never left him, and he could exag-

gerate it as many of the clergy were doing, but his eyes
were forward. He probably never met young Benjamin
Franklin, who would be twenty-four years old when
Sewall died, but the two might have had something to
say to each other.

When a man's work is done, his pen idle and his voice
still, his image somehow becomes simpler, as Henry
James once said. Perhaps also the meaning of his life
becomes more intelligible. As one looks back on Samuel
Sewall through a long vista, what unifies his life and
perhaps explains it (certainly it dominates his image) is
religion. It was not the religion of the first generation,
not John Cotton's or Thomas Hooker's or John Winthrop's. It was not the religion of Sewall's own younger
contemporaries, and not the religion of a later American
day. It was his own and it put its stamp on everything
he thought or did. When he awoke in the morning his
first thought was the Scripture lesson and the Psalm
for the day. To go to the Town-House or mount his
horse for the Court circuit without the family worship
would have been unthinkable to him. It is easy to dismiss
this traditional program as a mere pattern, but to look
twice is to see that for Judge Sewall, whatever the
pattern meant to him, it cannot be dismissed or subtracted. It was not separate; it cannot be subtracted; he
cannot be understood without it.

Once in a discussion at the Governor's Council about
a fast to be ordered, the Governor said, "Civil and religious Liberties," apparently a phrase to be inserted in
the Proclamation. "I said," Sewall reported, "Religious
was contain'd under Civil, arguing that Civil should go
first. Capt. Hutchinson said Religious should go first."
A moment in discussion; agree or not as one will, but
Samuel Sewall was unconsciously revealing something

fundamental in his own life. To him religious was included under civil, and under also whatever other areas
of life one may care to mention.

America was beginning to be bigger than New England before Sewall died. He belonged only to Boston,
which was also beginning to feel the enlargement. He
took pride in the newness. "Tis a great thing to be a
Foundation Stone in such a Spiritual Building as is now
to be erected in Newbury," he wrote to his young
nephew Henry Sewall. Foundation stones are not all
laid by the first generation in the first chapter of a nation's history. Nor are they all laid by giants among
men. Samuel Sewall was not a man of heroic stature in
an American hall of fame, but that is not important. He
was not one of the men ill at ease to whom the world
owes many of its onward impulses. Perhaps that is not
important either. Instead, he is one of those to remind
us that the work of the world, in superstructure as well
as foundations, then as now, is accomplished not only by
the labors of such as will be called great men.

As one looks back on this man of Boston in a far day,
one of the impressions that endures about him is suggested by the word one finds now and again applied to
him by those who knew him in Boston. "Good Mr.
Sewall," they said. With all his pride in high-sounding
titles, he might have liked it better than *Judge* Sewall,
or even *Captain*.

NOTES

ONE From These Roots (*pages 5–19*)

1. The quoted phrases are taken from a letter written by Samuel Sewall for his son, August 26, 1720, *Diary of Samuel Sewall*, Mass. Hist. Soc. Coll., Fifth Series, Boston, 1878–1882, 3 vols., I, Intro., XI–XV.
2. *Ibid.*, III, Memorandum, p. 396.
3. "Colonial Records," quoted by Joshua Coffin, *A Sketch of the History of Newbury, Newburyport and West Newbury*, Boston, 1845, pp. 14, 16.
4. *Ibid.*, p. 18.
5. *Diary*, I, Intro., XII.
6. Included in Thomas Hutchinson, *The History of the Colony and Province of Massachusetts Bay*, 2 vols., edited by Lawrence Shaw Mayo, Harvard University Press, Cambridge, Mass., 1936, I, 438.
7. John J. Currier, *The History of Newburyport, Massachusetts*, 1764–1909, 2 vols., Newburyport, 1909, II, Appendix, 580–583.
8. Henry Fitzgilbert Waters, *Genealogical Gleanings in England*, 2 vols., Boston, 1889, II, 1415–1416. The will was drawn May, 1628; proved, June 13, 1632. It is contained also in Edward Elbridge Salisbury, *Family Memorials*, 2 vols., New Haven, 1885, I, 153–158.
9. For an account of the Sewall forbears, with a pedigree, see Salisbury, *op. cit.*, I, 145–212; for a claim to the crest, see Colonel Chester's account *ibid.*, pp. 164–166.
10. *The Letter Book of Samuel Sewall*, Mass. Hist. Soc. Coll.,

Sixth Series, 1886–1888, 2 vols., II, 6–7. For an account of the Dummer heritage, see Salisbury, *op. cit.,* I, 215–280; a pedigree is included.

11. From his letter to his son, *Diary,* I, Intro., XII.
12. For details of Hampshire, see George Edward Jeans, *Memorials of Old Hampshire,* London, 1906, particularly "North Baddesley," by Rev. P. Gainsford Bourne, pp. 199–203 and "Romsey Abbey," by Rev. J. Cooke Yarborough, pp. 156–167.

TWO Orthodox School Days (*pages 20–29*)

1. *Diary,* July 6, 1715, III, 48.
2. For a contemporary sketch of Thomas Parker, see Cotton Mather, *Magnalia Christi Americana,* 2 vols., Hartford ed., 1820, I, Chap. XXV, entitled "Scholasticus," 433–435; also in Appendix, containing "Memoirs of Mr. James Noyes," 436–440. And see Samuel Eliot Morison, "The Education of Thomas Parker of Newbury," *Pub. Col. Soc. of Mass.* 1930–1933, Vol. XXVIII, 261–267.
3. Coffin, *op. cit.,* p. 69.
4. *Ibid.,* p. 64.
5. *Ibid.,* p. 66.
6. *Diary,* July 8, 1677, I, 43.
7. Coffin, *op. cit.,* pp. 66–67.
8. *Ibid.,* p. 65.
9. *Ibid.,* p. 64.
10. Quoted, *infra,* pp. 155–156.

THREE Harvard College (*pages 30–46*)

1. *Diary,* I, Intro., XIII–XIV.
2. From the entrance requirements as enlarged by the Overseers in 1655. See Samuel Eliot Morison, *Harvard College in the Seventeenth Century,* 2 vols., Harvard University Press, Cambridge, Mass., 1936, I, 81.
3. *Ibid.,* I, p. 85.

4. *Ibid.*, I, p. 84.
5. "Diary of Edward Taylor," *Mass. Hist. Soc. Proc.*, 1881, Vol. XVIII, 15.
6. Morison, *op. cit.*, I, p. 216.
7. *Old South Leaflets*, No. 51, 1895.
8. For a sketch of the members of the class of 1671, see John Langdon Sibley, *Biographical Sketches of Graduates of Harvard University*, Vol. II. Class of 1671.
9. Cotton Mather, *op. cit.*, under title, "Ecclesiastes," II, 54–96.
10. *Letter Book of Samuel Sewall, op. cit.*, I, 18.
11. Quoted, Morison, *op. cit.*, II, 547, note 2.
12. *Diary*, Dec. 3, 1673, I, 2. Adrian Heereboord (1614–1659) of Leyden, *Meletemata Philosophica* (Philosophical Exercises), 1654.
13. Quoted, Morison, *op. cit.*, II, 407.
14. *Diary*, October 16, 1674, I, 5–6.
15. Quoted, Morison, *op. cit.*, II, 408.
16. *Diary*, Nov. 24, 1674, I, 7.

FOUR   New Directions (*pages 47–65*)

1. "Memoir of John Hull," *Archeologia Americana, Transactions and Collections, American Antiquarian Society*, 1867, III, 125. See also Samuel Eliot Morison, *Builders of the Bay Colony*, Portland, Maine, 1940, p. 52.
2. *Ibid.*, pp. 53–67. The coins are illustrated.
3. *Ibid.*, p. 63.
4. "Diary of John Hull," *Archeologia, op. cit.*, III, 145–146.
5. *Ibid.*, III, 149.
6. And recalled it fifty-four years later.
7. *The Works of Nathaniel Hawthorne*, Boston, 1900, XI, 37–43.
8. *Archeologia, op. cit.*, III, Appendix, 274–275.
9. *Diary*, Jan. 6, 1676/77, I, 32; Feb. 23, 1676/77, 36; Dec. 21, 1676, 31–32; June 16, 1676, I, 14.
10. *Archeologia, op. cit.*, III, 124.

11. *Diary,* Feb. 7, 1676/77, I, 35. Translated in *Archeologia, op. cit.,* III, 253.

12. *Diary,* Apr. 4, 1675, I, 9.

13. In a letter to "Mr. Oates," Mar. 31, 1677, *Diary,* I, 39.

14. *Diary,* Mar. 21, 1678/79, I, 46, note.

15. *Diary,* Apr. 8, 1677, I, 40.

16. Thomas Parker died, Apr. 24, 1677.

17. *Letter Book,* Mar. 7, 1726/27, II, 223, memoranda, and *Records of the County of Suffolk,* 1671–1680, 1933, XXX, 1015.

18. The location of the house has been the subject of some difference of opinion. For a clear statement of what would seem to be a final solution, see Estes Howe, "John Hull and Samuel Sewall," *Mass. Hist. Soc. Proc.,* Nov. 1884, 2nd Series, I, 312–326.

19. *Archeologia, op. cit.,* III, 262, prints a copy from the *Records of Deeds for Suffolk County,* Lib. 13, fol. 92.

20. *Letter Book,* I, 282.

21. *Ibid.,* I, 325–326.

FIVE   Merchant Adventurer *(pages 66–78)*

1. "A Briefe Description of New England and the Several Townes therein, together with the Present Government thereof," *c.* 1660. The MS of this piece was discovered in the British Museum by Henry F. Waters; see Waters, *op. cit.,* pp. 14–15. It is also reprinted in *Mass. Hist. Soc. Proc.,* Oct. 1884, 2nd Series, I, 231–249.

2. For a general statement concerning trade at this time, see William B. Weeden, *Economic and Social History of New England,* 1620–1789, 2 vols., Boston and New York, 1890, I, 232–267, "The Working of the Navigation Acts."

3. For the text of the decree, see Herbert L. Osgood, *The American Colonies in the Seventeenth Century,* 3 vols., New York, 1907, III, 333–334.

4. The *Journal* is in the Baker Library, Harvard School of

Business Administration, Cambridge, Mass. See *Letter Book, op. cit.*, vol. I.

5. *Ibid.*, May 3, 1594, I, 141–142.
6. *Ibid.*, Sept. 9, 1699, I, 112; Apr. 11, 1695, I, 154.
7. *Ibid.*, Feb. 19, 1691/92, I, 129–130.
8. *Ibid.*, Apr. 5, 1687, I, 46; Nov. 10, 1687, I, 65; Dec. 1687, I, 75.
9. *Ibid.*, June 12, 1688, I, 84; July 10, 1688, 85–86.
10. *Ibid.*, Oct. 24, 1691, I, 123–124; Oct. 25, 1693, I, 139–140; May 16, 1699, I, 211.
11. *Ibid.*, Oct. 16, 1706, I, 338.
12. *Ibid.*, Oct. 24, 1693, I, 136–137. For additional itemized shipments, see *Mass. Hist. Soc. Proc.*, 1919, Vol. LII, 334–340.
13. For a recent authoritative statement and discussion, see Bernard Bailyn, *The New England Merchants in the Seventeenth Century*, Harvard University Press, Cambridge, Mass., 1955, especially Chap. VII, "The New England Merchants at the End of the Seventeenth Century."

SIX 'Twas Never So in Boston Before'
(*pages 79–95*)

1. Oct. 23, 1684.
2. *Letter Book, op. cit.*, Sept. 5, 1724, II, 173.
3. *Diary*, Apr. 1, 1686, I, 131.
4. *Ibid.*, June, 1685, I, 79–80; July 21, 1685, I, 89; Nov. 18, 1685, I, 106.
5. *Ibid.*, during last half of 1685.
6. *Ibid.*, June 20, 1685, I, 83.
7. *Ibid.*, Nov. 12, 1685, I, 103–104.
8. *Ibid.*, Dec. 25, 1685, I, 114.
9. *Ibid.*, May 17, 1686, I, 138–139.
10. *Ibid.*, May 21, 1686, I, 140.
11. *Ibid.*, May 26, 1686, I, 141.

12. *Diary*, June 5, 1686, I, 143.
13. *Ibid.*, June 7, 1688, I, 216.
14. *Ibid.*, Apr. 25, 1688, II, 20*, in Miscellaneous Items.
15. *Ibid.*, May 15, 1700, II, 13.
16. *Ibid.*, Aug. 20, 1686, I, 147.
17. *Ibid.*, May 26, 1686, I, 141.
18. *Ibid.*, Mar. 23, 1687, I, 171.
19. *Ibid.*, June 1, 1687, I, 179–180.
20. *Ibid.*, June 23, 1688, I, 217–218.
21. *Ibid.*, Mar. 28, 1688, I, 207.
22. *Ibid.*, July 12, 1688, I, 219.
23. *Ibid.*, Oct. 2, 1688, I, 228.
24. *Ibid.*, July 24, 1688, I, 237.

SEVEN   The English Journey (*pages 96–111*)

1. In a letter to Increase Mather in London, *Diary*, I, 229–230 note.
2. *Ibid.*, Aug. 15, 1688, I, 223–224.
3. In a letter to Edward Hull, Nov. 21, 1688, *Letter Book*, I, 92.
4. *Diary*, I, 237, 238, 240, 259, 237.
5. *Ibid.*, Dec. 2, 1688, I, 238–239.
6. *Ibid.*, Dec. 4–21, 1688, I, 239, 240.
7. *Ibid.*, Jan. 6, 1688/89, 243–246.
8. *Ibid.*, Jan. 14, 1688/89, I, 247, 293.
9. *Ibid.*, May 27, 1689, I, 256.
10. *Ibid.*, June 27, 1689, I, 260.
11. In his almanac record, *ibid.*, April 3, 1689, 303.
12. *Ibid.*, July 15, 1689, I, 265.
13. *Ibid.*, Oct. 5, 1689, I, 277.
14. *Ibid.*, June 28, 1689, I, 261.
15. *Ibid.*, Apr. 10, 1689, I, 305.
16. *Ibid.*, May 7, 1689, I, 254; May 18, 1689, 256.
17. *Ibid.*, Apr. 26, 1689, I, 251.
18. *Ibid.*, Nov. 20, 1689, I, 282.
19. *Ibid.*, Nov. 28, 1689, I, 284.

20. Quoted, Herbert L. Osgood, *The American Colonies in the Seventeenth Century*, 3 vols., New York, 1907, III, Chapter XIV, 418 ff.

21. On the title page the authors are stated to be "Several gentlemen who were of his Council." "To the Reader" is signed, E.R.; S.S. It is reprinted in Peter Force, *Tracts and Other Papers*, Washington, D.C., Vol. IV, No. 9.

22. *Diary*, April 21–May 9, 1690, 1, 317–320.

EIGHT   On the Bench in Salem Village

(*pages 112–136*)

1. In Plymouth's version of this law in 1671, the statute read, "If any *Christian* be a witch, . . ." The insertion of the word *Christian* was intended to save the Indians who were regarded as devil worshippers.

2. John Winthrop, *History of New England*, 2 vols., Savage edition, Boston, 1826, II, 326.

3. *Ibid.*, I, 315, 321. Also Hutchinson, *op. cit.*, I, 160–161; II, 13.

4. *Late Memorable Providences Relating to Witchcrafts and Possessions*, London, 1691; Hutchinson, *op. cit.*, II, 14–17.

5. March 10, 1664. An account of these trials was printed in London in 1682.

6. Samuel P. Fowler, *An Account of the Life, Character &c. of the Rev. Samuel Parris of Salem Village*, Salem. 1857.

7. Charles Wentworth Upham, *Salem Witchcraft*, 2 vols., Boston, 1857, II, 85, 86. This sermon was immediately published in London and reprinted in 1704.

8. *Ibid.*, II, 102–103, 108. For more texts of the examinations, see also Hutchinson, *op. cit.*, II, 19–31. Other records are listed in Marion L. Starkey, *The Devil in Massachusetts*, New York, 1949, Statement of Primary Sources, pp. 301–302.

9. *Op. cit.*, II, 107, 212.

10. *Diary*, Apr. 11, 1692; II, 358.

11. *Diary*, July 30, 1692, II, 362.
12. *Letter Book*, July 20, 1692, I, 132.
13. See also her "Humble Petition," Upham, *op. cit.*, II, 327–328.
14. For a summary view from another century, see Perry Miller, *The New England Mind from Colony to Province*, Harvard University Press, Cambridge, Mass., 1953, Chap. XIII, "The judgement of the Witches," pp. 191–208.
15. Upham, *op. cit.*, II, 509–512.
16. *Diary*, Sept. 21, 1692, I, 365; Sept. 22, I, 367; Oct. 29, I, 368.
17. *Ibid.*, Nov. 22, 1692, I, 369–370.
18. *Ibid.*, Dec. 19, 1696, I, 441.
19. *Ibid.*, Dec. 25, 1696, I, 443.
20. *Ibid.*, Jan. 16, 1696, I, 445.

NINE   On the Bench in the Superior Court
(*pages 137–151*)

1. *The History of Litchfield, Conn.*, Litchfield, 1900, pp. 98–109.
2. "Plaine Dealing or, Newes from New-England," London, 1642, reprinted in Mass. Hist. Soc. Coll., 3rd Series, 1833, III, 83–84.
3. *Letter Book*, I, 310–311.
4. *Diary*, Feb. 13, 1703, II, 73.
5. *Letter Book*, Aug. 5, 1700, I, 240.
6. *Diary*, May 2, 1709, II, 254.
7. For a brief statement, see John Noble, "The Early Court Files of Suffolk County," *Pub. Col. Soc. of Mass.*, III, 317–328. The 250,000 papers in the office of the Clerk of the Supreme Judicial Court of Suffolk County extend from 1629 to 1800. There is a thirty-volume index to this collection.
8. *Diary*, Dec. 1, 1705, II, 143; Nov. 15, 1720, III, 276–277.

9. Some details of this incident are given in a long note, *Diary*, II, 144–147.
10. *Diary*, Dec. 14, 1705, III, 148–149.
11. *Ibid.*, Jan. 2, 1722/23, III, 317–318. This speech was reprinted in the *Boston News-Letter*.
12. *Letter Book*, Jan. 2, 1717/18, II, 88.
13. *Ibid.*, Feb. 11, 1717/18, II, 89–90.
14. *Diary*, Mar. 11, 1726/27, III, 382.

TEN   *Phaenomena Quaedam Apocalyptica*
(*pages 152–156*)

1. 2nd. Edition, Boston, 1727, p. 45.
2. To Cotton Mather again, Aug. 4, 1713, *Letter Book*, II, 22. To Wadsworth, Feb. 3, 1725/26, *Letter Book*, II, 201.
3. *Ibid.*, Apr. 12, 1698, II, 197.
4. *Ibid.*, Aug. 22, 1728, II, 272–274.

ELEVEN   The New England Company
(*pages 157–161*)

1. For an account of a manuscript volume of the Company's records, see George Parker Winship, "Samuel Sewall and the New England Company," *Mass. Hist. Soc. Proc.*, 1941–1944, Vol. 67, 55–77. The Appendix to this article is an Index giving names of the persons who appear as having received payments, 1708–1719, with brief indications of the service rendered. For a recent book-length account of the work of the Company, see William Kellaway, *The New England Company*, London, 1961.
2. *Diary*, Jan. 24, 1703/04, II, 93.
3. *Letter Book*, May 3, 1700, To Sir William Ashurst, II, 231–233. Sewall mentions the necessity for "bounds" again in a letter to Jeremiah Dummer, Feb. 23, 1719/20, II, 108–110.

4. *Letter Book*, Apr. 13, 1706, To John Higginson, I, 326. See also a letter to Gov. Burnet, of New York, Sept. 23, 1723, "Whether God is not angry with the Country for doing so little toward the conversion of the Indians?" *Ibid.*, II, 156.
5. *Ibid.*, Sept. 26, 1687, I, 62; July 9, 1688; Dec. 3, 1690, Memoranda, I, 113. Letters to Edward Milton, carpenter, engaged to build the meetinghouse.
6. *Diary*, Jan. 2, 1700/01, II, 27–28. "The Bellman said these verses a little before Break-a-day, which I printed and gave them."

TWELVE 'The Selling of Joseph' (*pages 162–168*)

1. For a reprint of this tract, see *Mass. Hist. Soc. Proc.*, 1863–1864, Vol. 7, 161–165; for Saffin's answer, see *Pub. Col. Soc. of Mass.*, 1892–1894, I, 103–112 (unfinished) and *ibid.*, 85–102, a discussion of the occasion, etc.
2. Genesis, 37, 15–28.
3. Selected from the tract.
4. In this letter he speaks of reprinting "that Question" a year later in reply to a statement in the "Athenian Oracle." *Letter Book*, Apr. 3, 1706, I, 326.
5. *Diary*, June 22, 1716, III, 87.
6. *Letter Book*, July 20, 1719, II, 101.
7. *Diary*, Jan. 1, 1704/05, II, 121.

THIRTEEN Courtships (*pages 169–181*)

1. *Diary*, Oct. 15–19, 1717, III, 143–144.
2. *Ibid.*, Oct. 23, 1717, III, 144–145.
3. *Ibid.*, Feb. 19, 1717/18, III, 169–170.
4. *Ibid.*, June 9, 1718, III, 186.
5. *Ibid.*, Nov. 30, 1718, III, 206–207.
6. *Letter Book*, June 1, 1721, II, 133–134.
7. Hanging sleeves were detachable sleeves trimmed with

ribbon and lace; a detail of children's dress. He is using it
figuratively, as of old age.

8. *Diary*, Aug. 3, 1721, III, 290–291.
9. *Ibid.*, Nov. 7, 1720, III, 274–275. For the earlier details
   as noted, see pp. 262 ff.
10. *Ibid.*, Dec. 6, 1724, III, 345.

FOURTEEN   Layman of the Old South
(*pages 182–192*)

1. *Diary*, Nov. 28, 1710, II, 291.
2. *Ibid.*, Sept. 16, 1713, II, 397–398.
3. *Ibid.*, Mar. 2, 1717/18, II, 173–174.
4. *Ibid.*, Jan. 16, 1700/1701, II, 31.
5. *Diary*, Jan. 13, 1695/96, I, 419–420.
6. James Janeway's *Token* was first published in 1671.
7. *An Historical Catalogue of the Old South Church, Boston,*
   Boston, 1883. See also Hamilton Andrews Hill, *History of
   the Old South Church,* 2 vols., Boston, 1890.
8. *Letter Book*, Sept. 9, 1726, II, 211.
9. "Resign my Councillor's Place," *Diary*, May 27, 1725,
   III, 357–358.
10. *Letter Book*, II, 183–184.
11. *Diary*, March 3, 1726/27, III, 382.
12. Hill. *op. cit.*, I, p. 426.
13. *Ibid.*, I, p. 443.
14. Both sermons were printed immediately.

FIFTEEN   The Diary (*pages 193–204*)

1. Selected from several early Massachusetts almanacs.
2. The almanac for the English journey is included in *Diary*,
   I, 293–308.
3. *Archeologia, op. cit.*, III, 165–250.
4. Selected from the early pages, *Diary*, I, 1674.
5. *Ibid.*, Jan. 24, 1685, I, 118.

6. *Diary*, Jan. 15, 1715/16, III, 71.

7. *Ibid.*, Sept. 14, 1687, I, 188–189.

8. *Ibid.*, Oct. 2 and 3, 1711, II, 323, 324. This was the fire that burned the first Town-House.

9. Peter Thacher's funeral, Dec. 27, 1727, *ibid.*, III, 387–388.

10. *Ibid.*, Sept. 24, 1709, II, 263; Dec. 25, 1711, II, 330.

11. *Ibid.*, June 30, 1704, II, 109–110.

BIBLIOGRAPHICAL NOTE

Works of SAMUEL SEWALL:

At his death January 1, 1729/30, Samuel Sewall left his more important writings in manuscript, apparently with no thought of publication. Only what later times have called minor pieces had appeared in print. At present very little remains in manuscript. His extant writings include:

1. The *Diary*, consisting of three volumes, covering the years December 3, 1673, to October 13, 1729. There is one missing volume from March 1678/79 to June 4, 1685. Extant almanac portions fill in various gaps through the missing years. The extant *Diary* was published in three volumes, *Collections of the Massachusetts Historical Society*, Fifth Series, 1878–1882. A new edition, said to be in prospect, is sadly needed. The MSS are owned by the Massachusetts Historical Society.

2. *The Letter Book*, consisting of letters, copies, and memoranda of letters from February 16, 1686, to September 11, 1729, with various letters of Samuel Sewall, Jr. relative to the settlement of his father's estate, were published in two volumes, *Collections of the Massachusetts Historical Society*, Sixth Series, 1886–1888. The MSS are owned by the Massachusetts Historical Society. A few other letters have appeared, among them, "Letters of Samuel Lee and Samuel Sewall Relating to New England and the Indians," *Publications of the Colonial Society of Massachusetts*, Vol. 14 (1913), 142–186, including comments by George L.

Kittredge. A letter of Samuel Sewall to Nehemiah Grew appears on pp. 153–155 of this article. The MS. is owned by the British Museum, Sloane MSS 4067, fols. 140–141.

3. *The Commonplace books,* five small notebooks of sermon jottings in scattered entries throughout his life. Unpublished. The MSS are owned by the Boston Public Library. A small volume of MS sermon notes is owned by the Massachusetts Historical Society.

4. *Talitha Cumi,* or an Invitation to Women to look after their Inheritance in the Heavenly Mansions, c. 1711. Copied in somewhat condensed form from one of Samuel Sewall's notebooks, with comments by Dr. George E. Ellis, in his paper "Selections from the Letter Book of Samuel Sewall," *Massachusetts Historical Society Proceedings,* 1871–1873, Vol. XII, 380–384.

5. *Samuel Sewall's Business Journal,* Sept. 18, 1685–July 19, 1689. The MS is owned by the Baker Library, The Harvard School of Business Administration. Unpublished.

6. "A Memorial Relating to the Kennebeck Indians," Sept. 8, 1721, published in *Collections of the Maine Historical Society,* First Series, Portland, 1853, III, 351–353.

Writings published by SAMUEL SEWALL
during his life:

7. "The Revolution in New-England Justified" (with Edward Rawson), Boston, 1691.

8. *Phaenomena quaedam Apocalyptica ad Aspectum Novi Orbis configurata,* Boston, 1697.

9. "The Selling of Joseph," Boston, 1700.

10. "Proposals Touching the Accomplishment of Prophecies," Boston, 1713.

SELECTED BACKGROUND MATERIALS

Bailyn, Bernard   *The New England Merchants in the Seventeenth Century,* Cambridge, Mass., 1955.
Brattle, Thomas   Copy of a Letter, giving a full and candid account of the Delusion called Witchcraft. . . . *Massachusetts Historical Society Collections,* First series, V, 61–68, 1835.
Chamberlain, N[athan] H.   *Samuel Sewall and the World he Lived in,* Boston, 1885.
Coffin, Joshua   *Sketch of the History of Newbury, Newburyport, and West Newbury, 1635–1845,* Boston, 1845.
Currier, John J.   *History of Newbury, Massachusetts, 1635–1902,* Boston, 1902.
Ellis, George Edward   "Address on the Life and Character of Chief-Justice, Samuel Sewall, in Old South Church, Sunday, Oct. 26, 1884," Boston, 1885.
Fowler, Samuel P. (Ed.)   *Salem Witchcraft,* Boston, 1865.
Hall, Michael G.   *Edward Randolph and the American Colonies,* Chapel Hill, N.C., 1960.
Hill, Hamilton Andrews   *History of the Old South Church, 1669–1884,* 2 vols., Boston, 1890.
Hull, John   "The Diaries of John Hull," *Archaelogia Americana, Transactions and Collections of the American Antiquarian Society,* Boston, 1857, III, 109–265.
Hutchinson, Francis   *An Historical Essay Concerning Witchcraft,* London, 1718.
Hutchinson, Thomas   *An History of the Colony and Province of Massachusetts-Bay,* Ed. by Lawrence Shaw Mayo, Cambridge, Mass., 3 vols., 1936, II, 1691–1750.
Kellaway, William   *The New England Company, 1649–1776,* London, 1961.

Lodge, Henry Cabot   *The Last of the Puritans; the Sewall Diary*, New York, 1878.

Mather, Cotton   *Late Memorable Providences Relating to Witchcrafts and Possessions*, London, 1691.

Morison, Samuel Eliot   *Harvard College in the Seventeenth Century*, 2 vols., Cambridge, Mass., 1896.

Osgood, Herbert L.   *The American Colonies in the Seventeenth Century*, 3 vols., New York, 1904–1907.

Parrington, Vernon L.   *Main Currents in American Thought*, 3 vols., New York, 1927, 1930, I, 88–97.

Salisbury, Edward Elbridge   *Family Memorials*, New Haven 1885.

Shurtleff, Nathaniel B. (Ed.)   *Records of the Governor and Company of the Massachusetts Bay*, V, 1684–1686.

Sibley, John L.   *Biographical Sketches of Graduates of Harvard University*, Cambridge, Mass., 1881, II, 1659–1677.

Upham, Charles Wentworth   *Salem Witchcraft*, Boston, 1867.

Washburn, Emory   *Sketches of the Judicial History of Massachusetts*, Boston, 1840.

Weeden, William B.   *Economic and Social History of New England*, 1620–1789, 2 vols., Boston, 1890.

Whitman, Zechariah G.   *History of the Ancient and Honorable Artillery Company*, Boston, 1842.

Winship, George Parker   "Samuel Sewall and the New England Company," *Massachusetts Historical Society Proceedings*, 1941–1944, XLVII, 55–110.

Woodward, William Elliot   *Records of Salem Witchcraft*, copied from the original documents, 2 vols., Roxbury, Mass., 1864.

Index

Adam (a slave), 163
Adams, William, 39, 85
Addington, Isaac, 86, 124
Alden, John, 128
Allen, Joseph, 170
Allin, Daniel, 55
America, The, 98
Ames, William, 23, 42
Amiel, 202
Andros, Sir Edmund, 77; and
    Old South, 91–92, 93–94;
    revolution against, 106, 109–
    110, 110–111, 139, 195
Andros, Lady, 91
Anne, Princess, 102
Annesley, Dr., 104
*An Peccatum Originale sit &
    Peccatum & Poena*, 43
Appleton, Samuel, 124
Arbella, The, 2, 3
Assembly's Catechism, The,
    116
Ashurst, Sir William, 140, 157,
    157–158
Atwood, Judge, 166
Augustine, Saint, 203

B

Baddesley, 5
Barret, G., 198
Bartholomew, Mr., 9
Basing House, 19
Basingstoke, 19
Baxter, Richard, 5, 116
Baynes, Paul, 162
Belknap, Brother, 162, 163
Bellingham, Elizabeth, 176
Bill of Contrition (Sewall's),
    134, 135, 136
Bishopstoke, 5, 6, 12
Body of Liberties (Massachu-
    setts), 113, 114
Booth, Elizabeth, 118
Boston Artillery Company
    (South), 45, 88, 194
Bosworth, Edward, 8
Bowles, John, 39
Bradstreet, Anne, 60
Bradstreet, Simon (Governor),
    53, 89, 109, 110
Brattle, Thomas, 103, 176
Brattle, William, 60, 103, 105

227

Brewster, Margaret, 27
Bricket, Nathaniel, 186
Bridge, Thomas, 64
Brinsmead, Mr., 64
Brockballs, Anthony, 109
Brown, Madam, 172
Brown, Mary (of Newbury), 155
Browne, Joseph, 35–36
Brygden, Zechariah, 36
Bunyan, John, 61
Burbank, Thomas, 72
Burr, Aaron, 138
Burroughs, George, 118, 126, 127
Burton, Richard, 118–119
Business Journal (Sewall's), 69
Butcher, Elizabeth, 188
Byfield, Col., 171

C

Callender, Rose, 117
Calvin, John, 86
Carrier, Martha, 126
Cary, Mrs., 126
Certainty of the World of Spirits, The, 118
Charles II, 5, 49
Chauncy, Charles, 31, 34, 39, 42, 64
Chauncy, Israel, 64
Checkley, Deacon, 179
Christmas, 86, 200–201
Churchill, Sarah, 118
Clark, Captain, 97–98
Clark, John, 10
Clarke, Mr., 93
Cloyse, Sarah, 124, 125, 130

Coke, Sir Edward, 139; *Reports,* 145, *Statutes,* 146, 147
Coleman, Lydia, 176
Colman, Thomas, 110
Columbus, 177
Commentary on Ephesians, The, 162
Commonplace Books, 30
Confession of Faith, The, 60
Cooper, Mrs. (daughter of Samuel Sewall), 179
Cooper, Mr., 192
Cooper (sermons), 151
Corey, Giles, 128–129
Corey, Martha, 122
Corwin, Jonathan, 112–113, 124
Cotton, John, 3, 8–9, 80, 94, 104, 116, 207
Cromwell, Giles, 24
Cromwell, Oliver, 12, 17, 19
Cromwell, Richard, 12–13
Cutler, Dr., 169

D

Danforth, Addington, 167
Danforth, Master, 36
Danforth, Samuel, 39
Danforth, Thomas, 124, 132, 137
Davis, Capt., 94
Dean, Mr., 54
Denison, Madam, 172–173, 174, 180
Denison, William, 172
D'Ewes, Simon, 194
Discourse of the Damned Act of Witchcraft, 118

Domera, Henry de, 16
Dommer, John (of Overton), 16
Dommer, Matilda, 16
Drury, Amy, 117
Dudley, Joseph (Governor), 77, 83, 84, 86–87, 88, 95, 145–146, 163, 172, 173, 174
Dudley, Rebekah, 176
Dummer Academy, 17
Dummer, Alice, 11
Dummer, Capt. (of Swathling), 5–6
Dummer heritage, 15–17
Dummer, Jane (wife of Henry Sewall, Jr.), 11
Dummer, Jeremiah, 17
Dummer, Madam, 151
Dummer, Matilda, 16
Dummer, Richard, 7, 8, 9–10, 11, 16, 17, 106
Dummer, Stephen, 5–6, 7, 11, 16, 148
Dummer, Thomas Pyldrum, 16
Dummer, William, 17
Dunster, Henry, 34, 36, 39

E

Early Piety Exemplified in Elizabeth Butcher, 188
Easty, Mary, 130
Eliot, John, 60, 85, 158–159, 164
Elithrop, Mrs., 151
Elizabeth and Dorcas, 8
Elkins, Mr., 55
Endicott, Governor, 90

Ephemeris of Coelestial Motions, An, 60
Erasmus, 99
Evelyn, John, 194
Eyre, John, 176

F

Figes, Mr., 20, 21
Flint, Mr. and Mrs., 86
Foster, Isaac, 39
Foster, John, 60
Frary, Capt., 94
Fuller, Thomas, 15

G

Garrison, William Lloyd, 167
Gedney, Bartholomew, 86, 112–113
George Fox Digg'd out of his Burrowes, 60
Gerrish, Mr., 151, 170
Gibbs, Mary, 179–180
Gibbs, Robert, 179–180
Gillam, Mr., 96
Glanville, Joseph, 118–119
Glover, Goody, 116
Goodwin children, 115–116, 117, 129
Goodwin, John, 115–116
Gookin, Daniel, 41, 43
Goose, Isaac, 81
Gould, James, 138
Grandfather's Chair, 53
Graves, Thomas, 35
Great Chalk Pit, 19
Green, Joseph, 131
Green, Samuel, 60

H

Hale, Sir Matthew, 117, 126
Halley's Comet, 37, 60–61
Hampden, John, 17
Hampshire, 5, 18–19, 25
Harmony of the Gospels, 60
Harris, Beny, 98
Harriss, John, 48
Harvard College, 3; entrance
   test, 31; daily regimen, 32;
   living quarters, 32–33; tui-
   tion, 33–34; course of study,
   34–35; tutors, 35–36; de-
   cline, 38, 44–45, 195
Hathorne, John, 113, 124
Hawthorne, Nathaniel, 53
Heaven's Alarm to the World,
   60
Heerboord's Physics, 43
Henchman, Madam, 172
Henry VI, 114
Henry VIII, 114
Hibbins, Ann, 115
Higginson, John, 142, 166
Hirst, Grove, 170
Historical Catalogue, An, 189
*History of the Old South
   Church*, 191
*History of the Wars with the
   Indians*, 60
Hoar, Dorcas, 132
Hoar, Leonard, 42, 44–45, 52
Hobbey, Col., 167
Hobs, Mary, 5
Hogg Island, 94–95, 97
Hooker, Thomas, 104
Hubbard, Mr., 84
Hull, Edward, 71, 72, 73–74,
   75, 127

Hull, Hannah, 52–53, 54, 61–
   62, 169–170, 192
Hull, John, 45; arrival in Boston, 47; piety, 48–49, 51–
   52; business interests, 49–
   50; frugality, 55; death, 61;
   estate, 61–62; his Diary,
   197; mentioned, 64–65, 67,
   68, 69, 70–71, 76–77, 78,
   160, 170, 191
Hull, Judith, 61–62, 134, 192
Hull, Robert, 47–48
Hutchinson, Anne, 16, 41

I

Ive, John, 72

J

Jacob, George, 126
James I, 114
James II, 84
Janeway's *Token*, 188
Jaques, Henry, 26
John Indian, 119, 125, 130–
   131
Johnson, Samuel, 135
Jones, Margaret, 115
Juno, 177, 178, 179

K

King Philip, 45, 52, 158–159
King William, 122

L

*Late Memorable Providences
   Relating to Witchcrafts and
   Possessions*, 116

Lawson, Deodat, 120–122, 123
Lechford, Thomas, 138–139
Legg, Deliverance, 176
Leverett, President, 42, 172
Leverett, John, Governor, 60
Lewis, Mercy, 118
Love, John, 72
Loyd, Rebekah, 176

M

Mansion House, 47, 48, 56, 64, 97, 192
Manton, Dr., 99
Marion, Deacon, 172
Mary and John, 7–8
Mason, Mr., 86
Massachusetts Body of Liberties, 113, 114, 147
Mather, Cotton, 86; on cross in colors, 90; on Goodwin children, 115–117; 118–119, 129; on witchcraft victims, 127; letter to, 154; on Negroes, 162; at Sewall home, 169; at Son Joseph's ordination, 184; *Token*, 188; quoted, 200; prays at execution, 201; turns maid out in street, 202
Mather, Increase, made freeman, 59; History of Indian wars, 60; sermon, 81–82, 95, 107, 110, 127, 174; protests demand for Old South, 92; speech at ordination, 184
Mather, Richard, 30
Mather, Samuel, 39, 106
Maverick, Samuel, 66
Mayhew, Thomas, 158, 177

Medulla Theologiae, 42
Milk for Babes, 116
Mitchell, Jonathan, 40
Modell for the Maintaining of Students, 40
Moodey, Mr., 86
Moody, Cousin, 201

N

Nash, John, 5
Navigation Acts, 67, 195
New England Company, 157–161
New England's First Fruits, 3, 37
Newgate, Thomas, 95
Newton, Thomas, 139, 140
North Daddesley, 12, 18, 19, 20
Norton, John, 39
Norton, Mrs., 54, 92
Nourse, Rebecca, 122, 130
Noyes, James, 7–8, 23
Noyes, Mrs., 175
Nowell, Alexander, 35

O

Oakes, Dr., 169
Oakes, Urian, 45
Old College (Harvard), 32–33
Old South Church, 44, 48, 57–58, 78, 92–94, 182–185, 190–191
Oliver, 92
Oliver's Delve, 19
Ordway, Mr., 6

Orphan's Best Legacy, The,
192

P

Palmer, John, 110
Parker, Thomas, arrival in
America, 7–8, 9; schoolmas-
ter, 21–22, 23–24; men-
tioned, 31, 35, 55–56, 59,
153, 157
Parker-Noyes house, 21
Parris, Elizabeth, 118
Parris, Samuel, 119–120, 122,
124–126
Partrigg, Mrs., 141
Pemberton, Ebenezer, 183–
185, 202
Pepys, Samuel, 5, 194, 197
Perkins, William, 118
*Phaenomena quaedam Apoca-
lyptica ad aspectum Novi Or-
bis configurata,* 29, 152–156
Phipps, Samuel, 39
Phips, Sir William, 112, 124,
130, 131, 132
Pilgrim's Progress, 61
Plum Island, 155
Preston, Dr. John, 99, 100, 177
Prince, Thomas, 185, 192
Procter, Elizabeth, 124, 125–
126
Procter, John, 126
Prudent Mary, The, 2, 6, 45–
46
Putnam, Anne, 118, 124, 131–
132
Pyldrum, Richard, 16
Pyncheon, Major, 86

Q

Queen Elizabeth, 114
Quincy, Ann, 72
Quincy, Cousin, 134
Quincy, Edmund, 48
Quincy, Judith, 48, 50
Quincy, Uncle, 189–190

R

Randolph, Sir Edward, 66, 68,
69, 86, 92, 94
Randolph, Lady, 91
Rashly, Mr., 18
Ratcliff, Mr., 90–91
Rawson, Edward, 110
Reeve, Tapping, 138
Reyner, John, 54
Richard the Black Prince, 15
Richards, John, 137
Romsey, 19, 20
Rose Frigot, The, 87
Ruggles, John, 172
Ruggles, Widow, 172, 175
Russell, James, 124

S

Saducismus Triumphatus, 118
Saffin, John, 163
Saltonstall, Sir Richard, 7, 14
Saltonstall, Nathaniel, 112–
113
Sampson, Mr., 100
Savelle, John de, 15
Seaflower, The, 48
Sergeant, Peter, 112–113

Several Poems compiled with great Variety of Wit and Learning, 60
Sewall (of Coventry), 8, 106–107
Sewall (of Isle of Wight), 15
Sewall (of Northampton), 15
Sewall, Hannah (wife), 52–53, 61–62, 108–109, 169–170, 171, 191, 192
Sewall, Henry (great grandfather), 14, 15
Sewall, Henry (grandfather), 7, 8, 12, 13–14, 15
Sewall, Henry (father), 6; arrival in America, 7, 8, 9; land granted, 9–10, 11; marriage, 11, return to England, 12; minister, 12–13; return to Newbury, 13, 25, 28–29; death, 29, 89; mention, 149
Sewall, Jane (mother), 11, 29, 186
Sewall, John (of Essex), 15
Sewall, Margaret (great grandmother), 14
Sewall, Samuel (of Boston)
brothers: John, 7, 13; Stephen, 7, 13
daughters: Elizabeth, 97, 109, 170, 188; Hannah, 97; Judith, 188–189; Rebecca, 188; Sarah, 133, 134
sisters: Anne, 13; Dorothy, 13; Hannah, 7, 13; Jane, 7, 13; Mehitable, 13
sons: Henry, 97; Hull, 97; John, 58, 97; Joseph, 97, 174, 178, 180, 184–185, 188, 191, 192; Samuel, 97, 134, 192; Stephen, 97
Sewall, Samuel (of Boston), from Hampshire to Newbury, 5–6; parental heritage, 7–17; birth and baptism, 18; pupil in Thomas Parker's school, 20–22; influence of Thomas Parker, 23–24; boy life in Newbury, 24–28; seven years at Harvard, 30–45; ministerial offer, 46; meeting with John Hull, 47, 52–53; marriage to Hannah Hull, 53–54; beginnings of merchant interest, 54–55; religious unrest, 56–58; made freeman, 59–60; takes charge of printing press, 60–61; settles John Hull's estate, 61–62; an active merchant, 69–78; public office, 83–84; a conservative in troubled times, 82–85; resigns Captain's commission, 89–90; opposes Church of England worship, 90–94; applies for British land titles, 94–95; spends a year in England, 96–109; writes vindication for Andros rebellion, 110–111; made judge in Salem witch trials, 112–113; acts in current view of witchcraft, 113–114; makes public confession of error, 132–135; appointed judge of Superior Court, 137–138; rides the

Sewall, Samuel (*continued*) judicial circuit, 140–144; advocates various changes in the laws, 144; invokes authority of Sir Edward Coke, 146–147; appointed Chief Justice, 148–150; writes *Phaenomena* . . . 153–156; serves Indian cause in New England Company, 157–161; writes against Negro slavery, 162–167; first wife dies, 167–170; marries Widow Tilley, 174; second wife dies, 175; courts Mrs. Ruggles, 175–176; courts Madam Winthrop, 176–179; marries Mary Gibbs, 179–180; resigns public offices, 189–190; opposes rebuilding of Old South, 190–191; last illness and death, 191–192; his Diary, nature of, 193–195; its method, 198–199; quoted, 199–201; as self-revelation, 202–204; religion and, 207–208

Sewall, William (mayor), 15
Sharpe, Dr., 102
Sheldon, Susannah, 118
Shepard, Thomas, 37
Shrimpton, Col., 84, 85
Shrimpton, Jonathan, 179–180
Shute, Governor, 149, 174
Sibbes, Dr., 178
Sibley, Mary, 119
Smith, Capt., 86
Smith, Mr., 84
Smith, Samuel, 167

Society for the Propagation of the Gospel, 157
Sowle, Joseph, 95
Spencer, John, 10
Stoddard, Brother, 179
Stoddard, Solomon, 35
Stork, Cousin Mary, 106
Storke, Mr., 75
Stoughton, William, 83, 86, 95; commissioner, 111; judge in witchcraft trials, 112; belief in spectral evidence, 127; leaves court in anger, 131; consents to holding of fast, 133; made Chief Justice, 137
Swett, Steven, 27

T

Taylor, Edward, 33, 35, 39, 77, 189
Temple, Sir William, 49
Thacher, Peter, 39, 200
Thacher, Thomas, 60, 182
Tilley, Widow, 174–175
Tituba, 119, 122
Trowbridge, Thomas, 145
Threeneedles, Sarah, 201
Torrey, Mr., 54–55, 88
Tuckerman, John, 199

U

Usher, Bridget, 172, 176

V

Vane, Sir Harry, 10–11

W

Wadsworth (President of Harvard), 154
Wadsworth, Benjamin, 169
Walcot, Deacon, 118
Walcot, Nancy, 118
Walcott, Mary, 124, 125
Walley, Mr., 177
Walter, Mr., 151
Wardwell, Lydia, 26–27
Warren, Nancy, 118
Webster, Elizabeth, 27
Welch, John, 201
Weld, Thomas, 39
Williard, John, 126
Willard, Samuel, 59, 61, 91, 92, 97, 130, 133, 134, 182, 183, 188
William of Orange, 101, 110
Williams, Abigail, 118, 124, 125
Williams, Dr., 169
Williams, Elisha, 154

Williams, Roger, 60, 160–161
Willoughby, Mr., 171, 172
Wilson, John, 3, 30, 48
Winchester, John, 145–146
Winslow, Edward, 158
Winthrop, John, 2, 3, 11, 16, 52, 115, 207
Winthrop, John, Jr., 14, 36–37, 60, 172
Winthrop, Madam (Katherine), 172, 176, 180
Winthrop, Wait Still, 86, 110, 113, 137, 148, 176
Wise, John, 154
Witches, statutes against, 114
Wharton, Mr., 86
Wharton, Lord Philip, 107
Wheelwright, John, 41
White (of Old South), 172
Whittier, John Greenleaf, 205
Woodbridge, John, 175
Woodbridge, Martha, 175
Woodgreen, Capt., 6
Wyclif, John, 104